Intellectual Disabilities

Intellectual Disabilities

Charles J. Golden, Lisa K. Lashley,
Andrew Grego, Johanna Messerly,
Ronald Okolichany, and Rachel Zachar

MOMENTUM PRESS
HEALTH

MOMENTUM PRESS, LLC, NEW YORK

Intellectual Disabilities

First published in 2016 by
Momentum Press, LLC
222 East 46th Street, New York, NY 10017
www.momentumpress.net

ISBN-13: 978-1-60650-873-2 (paperback)
ISBN-13: 978-1-60650-874-9 (e-book)

Momentum Press Child Clinical Psychology "Nuts and Bolts" Collection

Cover and interior design by Exeter Premedia Services Private Ltd., Chennai, India

First edition: 2016

10 9 8 7 6 5 4 3 2 1

Printed in the United States of America.

Abstract

Clinicians within the fields of neuropsychology and school psychology may find this text to be a useful guide in understanding and assessing intellectual disabilities. This resource will provide information regarding the current status of diagnosis, conceptualization, and evaluative methods of intellectual disabilities. Interventions regarding the remediation of the various subtypes of intellectual disabilities and case studies will be provided. The focus of this resource is to provide clinicians and students with valuable information in the diagnosis, evaluation, and interventions regarding intellectual disabilities.

Keywords

evaluation and assessment of intellectual disabilities, intellectual disabilities, intellectual disability diagnosis, mild, moderate, neuropsychological assessment of intellectual disabilities, profound, severe

Contents

Chapter 1   Description and Diagnosis 1

Chapter 2   From Mental Retardation to Intellectual Disability:
             Current Conceptualization 5

Chapter 3   Evaluation and Assessment of Individuals with
             Intellectual Disability..27

Chapter 4   Intellectual Disability Recommendations for School
             and Work Settings 63

Chapter 5   Case Studies...71

References 129
Index 137

CHAPTER 1

Description and Diagnosis

Intellectual disability represents a multifaceted psychological, biomedical, and sociocultural construct that has a long-standing history of changing conceptualization, assessment, diagnosis, and treatment. The operational definition of disability according to Schalock, Luckasson, and Shogren (2007) is, "the expression of limitations in individual functioning within a social context and represents a substantial disadvantage to the individual" (p. 117). The diagnosis of intellectual disability describes a global deficit in cognition that impairs individuals from interacting with their environment in a meaningful manner. These deficits in cognition and adaptive functioning are observed during development and represent a significant discrepancy when compared to other individuals of the same age (Schalock and Luckasson 2013).

The term intellectual disability is a relatively new one. Individuals with the aforementioned cognitive and adaptive deficits were previously diagnosed with mental retardation to denote the delay in development. However, more recently, with the introduction of the fifth edition of the Diagnostic and Statistical Manual of Mental Disorders (DSM-5; American Psychiatric Association [APA] 2013), this term has been changed to intellectual disability, though the 10th revision of the International Statistical Classification of Diseases and Related Health Problems (ICD-10; World Health Organization 1992) continues to use mental retardation. Other current terms include: mental deficiency, mental handicap, mental subnormality, developmental disability, and learning disability (Schalock and Luckasson 2013). Terminology surrounding intellectual disability is important not only for clinical purposes, but also for the sociocultural implication that it carries, namely the weight of social stigma. Nomenclature, particularly surrounding intellectual disability, is so important because of the history of stigmatization and the limits that this label imposed. The current understanding, conceptualization, and nonmenclature of intellectual disability have taken hundreds of years to develop and are reflective of advances in research, and technology as well as the social mores and attitudes of the time with a more recent emphasis placed on a humanistic and community-based treatment (Harris 2006).

Severity and Diagnosis

To determine the diagnostic specifier of severity, the evaluation of adaptive functioning is necessary to determine the level of intervention that is needed. The diagnostic distinction between intellectual disability and borderline intellectual functioning is the presence of deficits in intellectual functioning but an absence of deficits in adaptive functioning, though no specific guidelines are presented for how to evaluate the discrepancy between cognitive and adaptive abilities. To determine the diagnostic severity of each individual, clinicians are directed to Table 1 on pages 34 to 36 of the DSM-5. If one or more deficits are observed in the conceptual, social, and practical domains in adaptive and intellectual functioning, then that individual is given the appropriate specifier. These specifiers should be evaluated according to the individual's age and corresponding appropriate developmental milestones.

Mild Intellectual Disability

According to the DSM-5, the diagnosis of mild intellectual disability is given when there are evident difficulties in acquiring and mastering academic skills (conceptual domain). In adults, deficits in neuropsychological domains of abstract reasoning, executive functioning, and short-term memory are observed. Individuals display immaturity in social interactions such as interpretation of nonverbal cues, difficulty in modulating emotions, limited understanding of social "risk" in interactions, and decreased social judgment. Notably, the authors caution that individuals in this category demonstrate significant gullibility, and are more prone to be easily controlled (social domain). Finally, the category of mild intellectual disability is assigned during childhood when more supervision is necessary to complete multistep activities of daily living than that of same-age peers. In adulthood, minimal support is needed for complex daily-living tasks, and for higher-order abstract processes ranging from transportation, grocery shopping, health care and legal decision, and raising a family. A vocation can be attained, though it should correspond to the individual's level of intellectual functioning. In general, there is minimal noticeable discrepancy between individuals with mild intellectual disability and individuals with an average level of functioning.

Moderate Intellectual Disability

Moderate intellectual disability is characterized by a marked delay in the learning of and mastering of academic skills, and requires outside support throughout an academic career. Academic development stalls and does not progress past elementary school (conceptual domain). A marked discrepancy is observed in same-age peers regarding social interaction and communication. Although the individual can have meaningful relationships, interactions are characterized by difficulty interpreting social cues, and communication is much more concrete as compared to that in same-age peers. Higher-order skills involving problem solving, planning, and decision making are markedly diminished and therefore the individual requires significant support in making all important life decisions (social domain). The individual with moderate intellectual disability is capable of performing basic personal hygiene and grooming, though it may take longer to master these skills, and even when he or she has mastered these, the individual may require prompting. Vocational attainment is possible though; like mild intellectual disability, it should correspond to the limited cognitive and communication abilities (practical domain).

Severe Intellectual Disability

Individuals with severe intellectual disability have significantly marked difficulty in comprehending rudimentary academic skills such as reading or counting. Higher-order abstract cognitive abilities do not develop and require caretakers to provide extensive support in making daily-life decisions (conceptual domain). Communication is significantly reduced as compared to same-age peers in terms of language production and vocabulary. Comprehension of language is only accomplished if short, simple phrases or words are used (social domain). Significant physical support is required to complete activities of daily living such as hygiene, grooming, and eating. While the individual with severe intellectual disability is capable of learning basic skills, this requires extensive teaching and prompting (practical domain).

Profound Intellectual Disability

Individuals with profound intellectual disability evidence minimal ability to manipulate their environment. They may be able to use objects to perform a simple task of self-care, work, and recreation (e.g., pushing a toy car or train). Individuals are likely to have comorbid motor and sensory deficits, which may further impair their ability to manipulate their environment (conceptual domain). Individuals do not demonstrate expressive language, and communicate primarily through gestures or other nonverbal cues. In terms of receptive language, they are capable of comprehending simple commands or words (social domain). Individuals with profound intellectual disability require full-time constant care and supervision for self-care and other activities of daily living. High levels of support are needed to complete basic recreational, skill-based, or self-care tasks.

CHAPTER 2

From Mental Retardation to Intellectual Disability: Current Conceptualization

The more recent change from the term mental retardation to intellectual disability is evidence of the continued shift in conceptualization and understanding. Perhaps, more than any other disorder or mental condition, the nomenclature used to describe a person with lower intelligence carries the implication of years of stigma and maltreatment. According to Harris (2006), "the continued use of this designation has been questioned because it implies a static, unchanging condition rather than one that can change over time" (p. 3). In addition, the mental retardation terminology has been criticized as being too circumspect, as only describing slowed mental processes, and does not describe the more complex etiological, functional, and neurobiological factors associated with intellectual disability (Ferguson, Ferguson, and Wehmeyer 2013).

Rather than the emphasis being placed on a person's innate deficit, the term intellectual disability and its accompanying conceptualization assert that the root of understanding the disability, is the person's cognitive functioning having a poor fit with his or her environment (Ferguson, Ferguson, and Wehmeyer 2013). The idea that intellectual disability is a medical condition is misleading; while it has biomedical contributing factors, the course is psychological and developmental with no "cure."

General intelligence is an artificial construct that reflects the general idea that we all have a basic level of functioning, which makes some of us intellectually faster or more able and others slower and less able. This parallels the concept of "g," a general factor that underlies all of our cognitive abilities. Originally, this type of intelligence was conceived to classify students in academic settings, with the goal of identifying those who were deficient and needed special classes or approaches and those who were abnormally good, also requiring a different approach. The idea underlying this was that those with higher intelligence quotient (IQ) would be more successful not only at school but in life in general, while those with lower IQ would be less successful.

Over time, it has become evident that such generalizations are not always true. Many individuals with high IQ are in fact less successful in life and even in academic settings, while others with lower IQ have happy and successful lives. The senior author was once asked by a major company to evaluate supervisors to see which ones were the most successful and whether this was related to intelligence or other cognitive factors. Over 50 supervisors were rated by the company on a number of internal criteria related to productivity, positive view of employees, ability to function within the company hierarchy, and so on. All were given a battery of IQ and cognitive tests. The results were very revealing. The IQs of the supervisors—all in the same job across different factories—ranged from 68 (technically at a level of mental disability) to 138 (genius level). However, none of the ratings of job success correlated significantly with the IQ measures. Some of the best supervisors were at the low end of the IQ evaluations, and some at the high end of IQ were at the low end of success. Clearly, there were factors that were much more focal than a general IQ, which predicted success (such as some personality factors, adaptive skills, problem solving under stress, emotional intelligence) much better than IQ.

So what use is IQ at all if we make this argument? Part of the problem is that we need to reconceive the meaning of IQ scores. Rather than representing an absolute level of function that predicts everything, an IQ should be regarded as an overall average ability. As an average, individuals' skills will tend to vary around the average primarily in a model that represents a normal curve. This means that about two-thirds of all of an individual's skills should fall within one standard deviation of the person's general IQ: Thus, if an individual has an average IQ of 100, scores for specific individual abilities should mostly cluster between 85 and 115 (if those scores of course are recalculated as standard scores rather than the t-scores, z-scores, percentiles, sten scores, stanines, and other scoring systems that are used to report data). This also means that the individuals will have about one-sixth of their skills at a level higher than 115 and one-sixth at a level lower than 85. One individual may show all of his or her skills in a relatively small range, but most of us will show distinct strengths and weaknesses across cognitive skills.

Because IQ is really an average rather than an absolute level, measurement of IQ is best done across a wide range of scores, which represent a range of distinct cognitive skills rather than a single score measuring one skill. While estimates for full IQs—especially in normal individuals—may be made by the use of a single test like Vocabulary skills or Matrix abilities on versions of the Wechsler Adult Intelligence Scale, such estimates may not be useful for those who show more variability in underlying skills. This is more likely to happen to those who are at the highest and lowest ends of the IQ continuum but can also occur in anyone regardless of their IQ. It should also be kept in mind that this range of skills only applies to cognitive skills and noncognitive skills such as sensory abilities and motor strength, dexterity, and speed are unrelated to general IQ, although motor or sensory tasks that also are cognitive tasks will more likely fall within the predicted scores based on IQ.

Primary Areas of the Brain

Thus, rather than thinking of severity as a single concept, it is best to assess whether an individual's overall classification represents a uniform distribution or one that conceals substantial strengths or weaknesses. One classification of skills may be based on Luria's (1976) concept of primary, secondary, and tertiary skills, each of which represents different areas of the brain although—like all abilities—they are interdependent on one another. The most basic skills of the brain are called primary abilities, skills that are foundational and generally built into the structure of the brain unlike the secondary and tertiary skills that are more a product of an interaction between the brain and the environment. Primary skills represent basic motor skills; basic sensory skills for hearing, seeing, touching, kinesthetic, and proprioceptive skills; and attention and concentration, as well as emotional reactivity and temperament. While all these basic skills are at least within normal ranges for most of us, this may not be true for individuals with intellectual disabilities.

Impairment in these basic skills has the impact of clearly delaying development after a child is born. The ability of evaluators to recognize a cognitive progress is severely impaired by deficits in these foundational skills. For examples, children with motor problems (often classified as cerebral palsy) will often appear to be intellectually disabled when in fact the cognitive areas of the brain are intact, something that can be seen only when an adequate motor response system to stimuli can be established. Similarly, children with hearing problems will be slow at developing speech, despite normal cognitive abilities.

This is complicated in that one may have motor problems and cognitive deficits at the same time, but it is difficult to determine which person is which. Even predictions made from neuroradiological tests like MRIs or CT scans can be misleading due to the fact that the injured brain can reorganize in a child to a remarkable degree, even when specific areas seem heavily damaged. The senior author saw one individual with over half his brain missing, according to a CT scan, who eventually developed above-average intelligence and skills despite "predictions" that he would always be impaired. While deficits in many of these areas are generally diagnosed by other professionals, individuals doing cognitive evaluations must be very much aware that such deficits (or strengths) may be present despite not being previously diagnosed.

Secondary Areas of the Brain

Secondary areas of the brain involve the cognitive integration of stimuli within a specific sensory or motor area so that we can learn to speak, understand, identify by touch, identify by vision, become aware of our own emotional states, and so on. Generally, each of these skills is mediated by specific areas within the brain that are dedicated to the processing of a specific type of stimulus and are "hard wired" to the specific primary areas dedicated to that modality. Thus, while primary areas can make certain visual or auditory discriminations from birth, these skills are also "hard wired" into the system and represent more of a reflex than a cognitive skill.

This same information is communicated to the secondary areas that are characterized by numerous, albeit random, and connections between neurons. Based on experience, learning takes place by reinforcing those connections that allow children to adapt, for example, by learning the sounds within their language through interaction with the environment. The presence of these numerous connections allows children to strengthen those connections that are needed, leading eventually to the discarding of those connections that are unnecessary. The presence of the connection at birth allows for quick learning at the secondary level rather than making the child to form new neural connections (as we may do as adults), which is a much slower method of learning. For this reason, learning as a child is very different from learning as an adult.

The connections that are reinforced differ from person to person, depending on the degree to which their environments differ. Those raised in similar environments will have more similarities at the level of neuronal interactions, while those from very different environments (learning English versus learning Chinese or a language based on clicks) will show much greater variations from one another.

The development of the secondary areas is dependent on both biology and environment, unlike the primary areas. Biologically, the individual's speed of learning will depend on the number of additional connections present and the speed at which the brain can respond to environmental stimuli in addition to the adequacy of the environment. The biological impact of injuries or failure of these areas to develop will differ based on plasticity, the area injured, and the severity. The environmental impact will depend on the adequacy of the environmental stimulation and feedback from the environment, such that impoverished or neglectful environments will lead to slower or overall poor development of the secondary areas.

The secondary areas can be classified roughly as motor, visual, auditory, and general sensory, the latter involving tactile, kinesthetic, proprioceptive, gustatory, and olfactory senses. In each case, there is a parallel right and left hemisphere secondary area, for a total of eight secondary areas across the cortex. The development of these areas may be at the same speed or may differ widely. For example, auditory-related skills may develop faster than visually or meteorically related skills. The adequacy of the development of the secondary areas depends as well on the function of the primary areas and the relevant sensory input. Visual areas will not properly develop if the eyes are not working or if the visual information is impacted by poor processing in the neural circuits leading to the primary area or in the primary visual areas themselves.

The concept of plasticity plays an important role in the outcome of injuries to the brain, especially in the pre- or postneonatal time periods up to about four to six years of age. Plasticity is the transfer of processes that usually takes place from one part of the brain to another part as a result of injury; the earlier the injury takes place, the more likely such a transfer will occur. In one case seen by the senior author, an infant lost prenatally an entire hemisphere, yet grew up to show perfectly normal cognitive skills as the remaining hemisphere took over all functions. Such takeover depends on the intactness of the remainder of the brain, the size of the injury, and the age of an injury, although no formula exists to estimate the likelihood of takeover in any given case.

The differences between the right and left hemispheres always play a role in determining the impact of an injury. In general (but not totally), the left hemisphere handles control and feedback from the right side of the body and the right side of each eye, while the right hemisphere controls the left side of the body and the left side of each eye. Importantly, though, the areas within each hemisphere handle cognitive processes differently. The right hemisphere appears to deal with novel stimuli, things that the person is unfamiliar with and patterns that are new or rarely repeated. It also plays a larger role in pattern analysis when those patterns are unfamiliar.

The left hemisphere is better at analyzing stimuli and motor processes that are overlearned and practiced. It is organized to repeat complex processes such as the understanding of speech and spoken language that require automaticity and speed. In such processes, one repeats sequences of analysis or motor actions over and over in the same manner. The left hemisphere is essential to the development of these automatic processes, which reflect much of our daily functions.

In young children, where everything that happens to them is new and novel, the role of the right hemisphere secondary areas is much greater than that in adults whose ability to analyze and respond is much more automatic. In a child with secondary impairment in the right hemisphere, the rate of new learning is slowed (or absent in extreme cases).

This impairment may arise as a result of injury or because of genetic or metabolic causes. This will lead to slowness in initial learning, which will appear similar to intellectual disability. Such deficits may initially be seen as developmental delays, as the child fails to reach appropriate milestones. The role of the environment in this process must also be considered. The development of the secondary areas appears to be fastest from birth until the ages of three or four years, so that early environmental deprivation can interfere with the development of these areas even in the absence of any injury. This can theoretically lead to inadequate development of these basic and important processing areas, which in turn will impact the development of intellectual and cognitive skills. After these critical periods, learning may come more slowly as the brain loses the additional connections relied on by the young child for quicker learning. Such individuals may need more intensive and repetitive training in order to try and make up for these deficits than would a normal individual, and the degree to which such interventions would be successful is unclear.

The difference between delay and long-term disability depends not so much on the initial presentation (although extreme cases may be clear) but on the long-term outcome, which is more unpredictable. One major factor is the intactness of the left hemisphere areas. As noted earlier, the left hemisphere functions best with overlearned sequences. When the right hemisphere is impaired, early learning will be slow (varying in severity) but often takes place, albeit over a longer period of time. If the left hemisphere is intact; however, this material will eventually be learned and the child will appear to catch up with others (although he or she may have lifelong struggles with a novel material). If the left hemisphere is also impaired; however, this will not take place and the individual will show more chronic disability.

In the opposite case, in which the left hemisphere is impaired but the right hemisphere is intact, we get a different picture. In such cases, early learning takes place normally, but problems begin to show up because the new learning never becomes overlearned. Intellectual levels will decline as testing expects more new learning, especially in prekindergarten and similar experiences. Failure of all secondary areas to develop due to severe injury or genetic disorders will lead to serious intellectual disability.

Tertiary Areas of the Brain

The tertiary areas of the brain represent the highest developed areas of the brain that most uniquely distinguish the human brain from those of other species. There are two tertiary areas: one located in the posterior of the brain in the parietal–occipital–temporal overlap (tertiary parietal area) and the other in the most anterior area of the brain in the frontal lobes (prefrontal area). The prefrontal area does not play a role in the diagnosis or etiology of mental disability, although it does play a major role in the development of executive functions and personal controls characteristic of adults. The tertiary parietal area, however, plays a major role in childhood and later academic and intellectual processes, with an especially important developmental time somewhere in the six- to ten-year age range.

The tertiary parietal areas (one in the right hemisphere and one in the left hemisphere) receive input from each of the secondary areas. While the secondary areas are responsible for foundational academic, speech, verbal, and nonverbal skills, the integration of these abilities into full-fledged academic and intellectual performance takes place within the tertiary parietal area. This allows the transition from the basic skills of the five- or six-year-old to the more complex skills of the middle or high school students. Failure of these areas to develop normally has a major impact on intelligence and school performance. If, however, the deficit is restricted to the tertiary areas, development will appear normal through at least the early school years.

If the injury is limited to the right hemisphere area, learning is delayed but with practice the child will be capable of catching up. Long-term problems will show up in tasks involving spatial analysis (from video games to complex eye—hand coordination to visual—spatial performance) and may surface in the understanding (but not the memorization) of advanced arithmetic relationships. Injuries to the left hemisphere, however, result in a lack of overlearning, which has the impact of impairing academic performance and complex verbal skills, all of which need to be automatic in order to be effective. Impairment in this area will lead to poor school grades and lowered IQ, generally in the borderline range (70 to 84) or in the mild intellectual disability range.

It should be noted that in cases in which there is a delay in the development of the tertiary areas, there will be a learning delay but this is correctable once the area develops. Late tertiary developers do not appear uncommon in working with children six to nine years old and may run in families as well, observationally more often in males than females. It is also important to note that learning will not take place, even in a biologically intact brain, without sufficient environmental training and feedback.

Finally, most skills described here as secondary skills are described elsewhere as crystallized skills. Tertiary skills may be classified as crystallized when overlearned and fixed and fluid when more complex and novel.

Etiology

Biological disorders or injuries associated with the development of intellectual disability can occur in the prenatal, perinatal, and postnatal periods. However, the cause of an individual's intellectual disability is often unknown (Maulik and Harbour 2010). Prenatal characteristics include genetic (i.e., Down's syndrome), congenital malformations, and exposure to teratogens (Maulik and Harbour 2010). Perinatal factors include infections and head-related trauma associated with birth; postnatal factors consist of early infection and deficiencies in development along with head injuries. Infections may involve neurological disorders such as encephalitis or meningitis or can reflect system infections arising from viruses or bacteria. Metabolic disorders can impair functioning of the body as a whole but, in some cases, may be potentially treatable. For diagnostic accuracy, however, it is not necessary to identify the etiology, but a good history identifying the etiology can help families identify genetic disorders so that families are aware of their presence and can help understand the likelihood of future cases. In many cases, the etiology is more in the interest of science and future clients than the current client, except in those rare cases in which the disorder is reversible.

Diagnosis

The history and sociocultural background surrounding the treatment of those with intellectual disabilities is primarily characterized by a lack of understanding, ignorance, and stigmatization. Ancient Egyptians are credited to be among the first to document the presence of persons with intellectual disability; ancient Greeks and Romans believed that those with disabilities were evidence of god's disfavor (Harris 2006). It has been a common belief that infanticide was employed in antiquity as a means of physically removing those with intellectual disabilities from the environment, though this has been challenged to assert that familial rejection was more common (Berkson 2004).

Throughout the middle ages, there were a wide range of beliefs surrounding people with intellectual disabilities; some believed that they were the product of demonic possession, some of which were treated with beatings of the head (Bromberg 1975). Others equated those with an intellectual disability patients with physical infirmities, believing that disabilities were attributed to the natural process of life's difficulties that indiscriminately affected some and but not everyone (Braddock and Parish 2001). Those with disabilities were classified with the poor, and were placed in designated institutions (Harris 2006). The legal term "idiot" was used to classify an individual who was considered cognitively incompetent from birth (Wickham 2013).

During the early 1600s, the onset of placing scientific thought at the forefront of understanding harkened a transition away from asserting that the individual with an intellectual disability was the product of religious or supernatural causes. It was in this era that it was hypothesized that the cause of intellectual disability was, at least in part, hereditary, and that the course was incurable (Wickham 2013). Importantly, intellectual disability was differentiated from mental illness as researchers, scientists, and leaders observed that the onset of mental illness was acquired later in life, whereas individuals with lower levels of intelligence were born with this characteristic (Braddock and Parish 2001). In England, people with intellectual disabilities were financially supported by the Poor Law of the government if the family was not able to care for them, though it is believed that this policy negatively impacted this population, as it began the stigma of being an unwanted burden on society (Harris 2006).

The 19th century established the foundation for the current standard of care and support for those with intellectual disabilities (Ferguson 2013). The term idiot began to fall out of favor, and was replaced with feeblemindedness (Ferguson 2013). Researchers and leaders saw the need for a system of classification, and long-term care, which was supplied by almshouses. However, individuals with intellectual disabilities still predominantly received long-term care from their families. The almshouses were also homes to the poor, older adults, and physically disabled, and were not designed to provide long-term rehabilitative care, or interventions (Ferguson 2013). The goal of these institutions was not to treat or remediate the individual's functioning: It was to remove them from society (Ferguson 2013). The stigma of the individual with an intellectual disability as being a drain on resources was perpetuated.

In the 1900s, science began to transform the way intellectual disability was conceptualized and named. It was during this time that the terms imbecile and mental deficiency were used, in addition to feeblemindedness. This historical change in nomenclature is important because it reflects a classification of the intellectually disabled as having a condition that is attributed to a deficiency in mental functioning rather than assigning a term that simply signified that the person was different from society in general (Wehmeyer, Noll, and Smith 2013). The idea that slowed or delayed mental processes could have a basis in biomedical causes was new and shifted the direction of research and classification. When it was thought of as a medical condition, a treatment, or rehabilitative process could be implemented. However, the belief that those with intellectual disabilities were dangerous, criminal, or lacking in moral fiber persisted, and segregation from society in the form of institutions that lacked treatment or care continued to be common (Wehmeyer, Noll, and Smith 2013). Adding to this, eugenics and the idea of racial purity was on the rise, and laws allowing involuntary sterilization were passed. The intent was to prevent the spread of diseases as it had been determined that intellectual disability was an inherited disease. The practice was employed on criminals and those with intellectual disabilities alike (Wehmeyer, Noll, and Smith 2013). An estimated 64,000 sterilizations were performed in the United States from 1907 to 1963 (Harbour and Maulik 2010; Radford 1991; Sofair and Kaldjian 2000).

Individuals with suspected lower levels of intelligence were first assessed by Binet and Simon (1913), who were commissioned by the French minister of public instruction who asserted that any student who was suspected of lower levels of intelligence should undergo a formal evaluation to demonstrate that traditional education would not be of benefit

(Binet and Simon 1916). The goal was to first identify children who could not benefit from the same instruction as normal children due to their innate level of intelligence, and to quantify that discrepancy before removing them from the classroom, and making appropriate residential determinations. While this helped with diagnosis, it is believed that this further increased segregation through institutionalization, as there continued to be no formal treatment or remediation mechanisms in place. This was the first instance of identifying a client with an individual disability and classifying him or her in a systematic way, rather than just through behavioral observation alone. Intelligence testing was continued and mainstreamed with its use in World Wars I and II to assign soldiers to jobs in the armed forces according to their intelligence (Beirne-Smith, Patton, and Kim 2006; Harbour and Maulik 2010; Radford 1991). Therefore, the modern basis of understanding and classifying individuals according to their level of intelligence and to identify those with an intellectual disability is in assessment.

It is only in the last 60 years that legal rights have been given to those with intellectual disabilities. The framework for long-term care has shifted to education and supportive rather than institutionalization (Harbour and Maulik 2010). As history demonstrates, the diagnosis or label of mental retardation or intellectual disability carries much weight. Throughout history, people have been scared of, distrusting, or resentful of persons with perceived lower levels of intelligence, and even more predominantly, they have been unsure how to classify, diagnose, and treat them. The history of the treatment of individuals with intellectual disabilities demonstrates that intelligence in general is a construct that operates within the confines of that particular sociocultural context. This is important to note as clinical psychologists assess for a person's intellectual capacity; consider the ramifications of this diagnosis; and direct the course of intervention, rehabilitation, and treatment. The current definition of intellectual disability according to the American Association on Intellectual Developmental Disabilities (2010) asserts that the accepted three criteria for the diagnosis of intellectual disability are: a deficit in cognitive functioning, a deficit in the ability to adapt to the environment, and the onset is before age 18 years.

History of DSM Diagnoses

The history of the diagnosis of intellectual disability through the seven editions of the Diagnostic and Statistical Manual of Mental Disorders (DSM) describes a long-standing difficulty in attempting to quantify and categorize the severity of below-average intellectual functioning. However, a diagnosis of intellectual disability presented a diagnostic issue: with such a broad term, the diagnosis of mental deficiency or mental retardation or intellectual deficiency was clinically meaningless. Not only is the presentation heterogeneous, ranging from mild to profound impairment, but also the etiology is quite varied, ranging from genetic to acquired. With the beginning of the use of standardized assessments of intelligence, the opportunity arose to establish a system of categorization that clinicians and researchers could use to first identify and create interventions or programs of remediation. The creators of the DSM learned from the aforementioned long and convoluted history that a diagnosis of subnormal intelligence cannot be made on observation alone, nor can it be assigned from solely a measure of intelligence. The history of the DSM with regard to the diagnosis of intellectual disability is marked by a wrestling between these two characteristics as well as determining the diagnostic criteria and cutoffs of IQ scores and the accompanying functional impairment.

DSM-I

The first edition of the DSM was published in 1952, and was the answer to the need to formally categorize and classify mental disorders. Mental disorders were categorized according to their etiology (American Psychiatric Association [APA] 1952). Furthermore, as the preceding discussion on the history of the terminology used to describe intellectual disability demonstrated, the authors asserted that the nomenclature used to describe mental disorders or conditions was vital for unity with the professional practice of psychology (APA 1952), and for education of the general public. The diagnosis of mental deficiency was used to denote an organic brain syndrome with a resulting deficit in global intelligence observed since birth and without a known cause (APA 1952). This diagnosis was reserved for intellectual deficits that were determined to be hereditary or idiopathic (APA 1952). This DSM established a similar categorization of deficits that became the basis for the modern classification primarily according to the individual's IQ accompanied by consideration of adaptive abilities. *Mild* was used to refer to an IQ range of 70 to 85, with an accompanying adaptive impairment in vocation. *Moderate* was used for an IQ range of 50 to 70 with observed functional deficits that require significantly more supervision and training. *Severe* denoted an IQ below 50 with significant impairment in activities of daily living, requiring total care. While the DSM-I made important strides in removing the use of emotionally charged words such as idiot, imbecile, or feebleminded, as well as creating a standardized, clinical method of organizing those with global deficits, this method did not speak to the complexity of intellectual disability, paving the way for the second edition of the DSM (DSM-II; APA 1968).

DSM-II

In response to the concerns of an insufficient description and classification of intellectual disability, the DSM-II altered the classification of what was renamed as mental retardation after consulting the American Association on Mental Deficiency (APA 1968). Notably, this edition sought to agree on a diagnostic terminology and description that would be accepted by international professionals. The definition of mental retardation was, "subnormal general intellectual functioning which originates during the developmental period and is associated with impairment of either learning and social adjustment or maturation or both" (APA 1968, 14). The basis of the diagnosis remained the same—that it should be based on a psychological assessment that demonstrated lower than average intelligence with accompanying adaptive and functional deficits. However, this edition sought to create a classification of deficits according to the statistical distribution of IQ scores in a normal population.

The ranges as set forth in the DSM-II were reflective of a standard deviation of 15 from the mean of 100. The classification of Borderline mental retardation ranged from an IQ of 68 to 85; mild mental retardation denoted an IQ range of 52 to 67; moderate mental retardation denoted a range of 36 to 51; severe mental retardation referred to an IQ range of 20 to 35; and profound mental retardation denoted an IQ of 20 and under. Unspecified mental retardation was given as a categorization of individuals who clearly evidenced deficits in intellectual functioning, but were unable to be formally assessed. This classification remained throughout the following editions. In addition, diagnostic clinical subcategories were added to classify the etiology of mental retardation with optional designations of following infection and intoxication, after a trauma or a physical agent, associated with gross brain disease or chromosomal abnormality. This method of classifying the physical etiology of the intellectual disability was likely quite cumbersome and did little to add to the understanding of the clinical manifestation of the diagnosis.

DSM-III and DSM-III-R

The third edition of the DSM was published in 1980 and introduced the multiaxial diagnostic system. One of the primary reasons for creating the multiaxial system was to create a holistic representation of the individual's functioning. The concern was that a clinician would become so focused on the primary presenting problem, likely an Axis I disorder, and disregard personality, intellectual, medical, and psychosocial characteristics (Black and Grant 2014). Therefore, one of the bases of constructing the multiaxial system was to include intellectual disability in the clinical consideration of the individual. Like the previous editions, the essential features of the diagnosis were subnormal intelligence and the presence of adaptive and functional deficits. The added third feature specified that the onset had to be before age 18 years. Significant below-average intelligence was broadly defined as an IQ score of 70 or below as determined by intelligence tests. Adaptive behaviors were defined as the ability of the individual to meet expected levels of social and independent functioning according to culture and age (APA 1980). While the use of a scale or measure to assess adaptive functioning was recommended, caution was given for the use of solely one measure to assess this area. The specification of 70 was assigned as the cutoff, as the authors asserted that adaptive functioning was significantly impaired at that level of intelligence as it fell two standard deviations below the accepted score of average intelligence (APA 1980). Importantly, individuals with IQ scores of 71 to 84 were no longer assigned a diagnosis of mental retardation; rather, they were given a V code of Borderline Intellectual Functioning. This diagnosis was assigned solely on the basis of IQ scores as no adaptive deficits were hypothesized to be evidenced.

The ranges of the classification of levels of severity are as follows: *Mild Mental Retardation* was given an IQ range of 50 to 70; *Moderate* referred to an IQ range of 35 to 49; *Severe* denoted a range of 20 to 34; and *Profound* referred to an IQ score of 20 and below. In terms of adaptive classification, Mild Mental Retardation was defined as "educable," meaning that these individuals would display minimal impairment in social, communication, and sensorimotor skills in preschool years and were capable of comprehending academic information up to a 6th-grade level (APA 1980). Moderate Mental Retardation referred to the category of individuals who were "trainable," those who needed vocational training, and required mild-to-moderate supervision and guidance. Severe Mental Retardation denoted minimal to no meaningful speech, and requiring extensive supervision. Profound Mental Retardation was defined as a minimal capacity for sensorimotor functioning and requiring constant supervision and assistance in activities of daily living.

The 1987 revision of the DSM-III highlighted the five-point error of measurement that accompanies the evaluation of intelligence using IQ ranges of 50 to 55 to approximately 70 for Mild Mental Retardation, 35 to 40 through 50 to 55 to describe Moderate Mental Retardation, 20 to 25 through 35 to 40 to refer to Severe Mental Retardation, and below 20 to 25 to describe Profound Mental Retardation (APA 1987). This subtle shift emphasized the importance of adaptive functioning: that if the IQ score was in the intersection between two levels of severity, the assessment of functionality and impairment was the ultimate determining factor in determining the severity of diagnosis. It also accentuated that intellectual disability's course is not a static, and rigid, particularly with regard to adaptive functioning that with remedial and treatment efforts, functioning could significantly improve (APA 1987). It was recommended that the assessment of adaptive functioning consists of a combination of a third-party observation, a review of medical and educational history, and the administration of accepted behavior scales.

DSM-IV *and* DSM-IV-TR

The fourth edition of the DSM in 1994 did not bring significant changes to the diagnostic conceptualization of Mental Retardation. The cutoff of IQ score of 70 (Criterion A) and the age of onset before 18 years (Criterion C), as set forth in the DSM-III-TR, were maintained. The degrees of severity of intellectual impairment remained the same from the previous edition. However, the diagnostic description of adaptive functioning (Criterion B) received some much-needed clarification. In addition to the subaverage intelligence scores, concurrent deficits needed to be observed in two areas of functioning: communication, self-care, home living, social or interpersonal skills, use of community resources, self-direction, functional academic skills, work, leisure, health, or safety (APA 1994). No changes were made to the DSM-IV-TR's 2000 edition with regard to Mental Retardation from the DSM-IV.

DSM-5: *Current Description and Diagnosis*

The DSM-5 created many ripples throughout the psychological community at large. It is of particular interest that the multiaxial diagnostic system was removed, with all psychiatric diagnoses listed according to the order of clinical significance of the individual. As previously mentioned, the diagnosis of Mental Retardation was replaced with Intellectual Disability. Intellectual Disability is included in the category of Neurodevelopmental Disorders, which is a renaming of the category of Disorders Usually First Diagnosed in Infancy, Childhood or Adolescence. It is included with diagnoses of communication disorders, autism spectrum disorder, attention-deficit or hyperactivity disorder (ADHD), neurodevelopmental motor disorders, and specific learning disorder. One of the goals of the DSM-5 was to create a conceptual structure of diagnoses, with the category of disorders listed first reflecting earlier age of onset.

The name itself was changed for several reasons. First, of primary importance, it is a term that is reflective of the advances made in the scientific understanding of the condition, and addresses the complexity of the disorder. The term mental retardation was deemed stigmatizing and therefore lost its use as being clinically relevant. In addition, starting in 2010, the designation of intellectual disability was used in U.S. law (Rosa's

Law) as well as professional journals (Black and Grant 2014). With the upcoming release date of the 11th Revision of the International Classification of Diseases in 2018, which was also going to make the transition to the usage of the term intellectual disability, it was deemed important to concurrently use the same diagnostic term (Black and Grant 2014).

However, the most important change surrounding intellectual disability is the redefinition of the disorder itself. The diagnosis is still made on the combination of objective, standardized testing, and clinical observation. However, the DSM-5 emphasizes the impact of functional impairment in the individual's ability to adapt to his or her environment rather than the IQ in determining the severity of the diagnosis. This is clearly observed in the complete removal of IQ scores to determine the severity of intellectual deficits, the most outstanding change to this diagnosis. This emphasis echoes the reconceptualization of intellectual disability as having a flexible and fluid progression over a static course, and implies that if an individual were to receive appropriate therapeutic and rehabilitative services, his or her ability to relate to the environment would increase, improving adaptive functioning, and reducing the severity of the disorder. This is reflective of an overall trend in the DSM-5 to emphasize diagnostic dimensions of disorders rather than relying on a checklist of yes or no to determine if the individual meets criteria or not (Black and Grant 2014). The burden of the diagnosis therefore rests more on clinical judgment in categorizing adaptive functioning rather than relying on standardized test scores. Objective assessment of both intelligence and adaptive functioning is highly important, but the interpretation of those scores and how they are representative of the individual's daily functioning is crucial.

The deficits in intellectual and adaptive functioning should be observed in three domains: conceptual, social, and practical to determine current severity. Conceptual functioning is defined, as considered general cognitive functioning. Social functioning is the ability of the individual to engage in reciprocal interaction with others, which involves the recognition of emotions in themselves and others, the ability to use communication skills, and social judgment. Practical functioning is the ability to independently adjust one's behavior according to the demands of society, which involves management of finances, vocational skills, and education.

As with previous DSM editions, Criterion A of the diagnosis speaks to the intelligence component of the diagnosis. The term intelligence is described by general mental abilities, which is defined as, "reasoning, problem solving, planning, abstract thinking, judgment, learning from instruction and experience, and practical understanding" (APA 2013, 37). This is subsumed under the domain of conceptual functioning. As with previous versions of the DSM, below-average intelligence is considered two standard deviations (30 points) below the mean of standardized tests of intelligence such as the Wechsler Intelligence Scales or the Stanford Binet Intelligence Scales. When considering scores of intelligence, the authors of the DSM-5 caution that IQ scores can only speak to domain of conceptual functioning, and may not be an accurate representation of the individual's ability to employ reasoning in social or practical domains (APA 2013).

Criterion B defines deficits in adaptive functioning as a "how well a person meets community standards of personal independence and social responsibility in comparison to others of similar age and sociocultural background" (APA 2013, 37). Unlike previous editions, the deficit has to be observed in at least one of the previously described three domains (e.g., communication, independent living, and so on). These deficits must be directly caused by the deficits in general mental ability. It is recommended that when considering Criterion B, clinicians consider personal observations, third-party or informant report (e.g., family, teacher), clinical interview, standardized measures of adaptive behaviors (e.g., Adaptive Behavior Assessment System), and review of records (e.g., medical, education, mental health).

Criterion C speaks to the age at which the deficits are observed. However, instead of broadly saying that the deficits need to be observed prior to the age of 18 years, the DSM-5 states that the onset must be during the developmental period, which is defined as being present during childhood or adolescence. Essentially, the constraints of observation are reserved from childhood to prior to the age of 18 years. This distinction is important as the current DSM now includes a new diagnosis of Global Developmental Delay, which is given only for children who are under the age of five years, and who fail to meet developmental milestones with regard to intellectual functioning. The reasoning behind the creation of this diagnostic category is that children under this age are too young to receive standardized testing, and therefore should be assigned a diagnosis of intellectual disability without an objective measure. This category of individuals would require formal assessment once they can be reliably and validly evaluated to clarify diagnoses. The diagnosis of unspecified intellectual disability is reserved for individuals over the age of five years who are unable to be undergo a standardized intelligence assessment due to other comorbid medical or psychiatric conditions.

Differential Diagnoses

Common differential diagnoses for intellectual disability include neuro-cognitive disorders, communication disorders, specific learning disorder, and autism spectrum disorder. Neurocognitive disorders are reserved for individuals who demonstrate a significant loss of intellectual function-ing due to a medical condition or insult. However, intellectual disability can be comorbidly diagnosed with a major neurocognitive disorder if the individual's current functioning is reflective of a significant loss of pre-vious functioning, and if intellectual disability was diagnosed prior to the insult.

Intellectual disability is differentiated from communication and learn-ing disorders in that broad, global intellectual deficits accompanied by adaptive functioning deficits are not observed. The individual with either one of these two disorders are able to independently carry out activities of daily living. Deficits are observed during specific situations which require communication skills. These deficits can include such as difficulties in the physical production of language (articulation, stuttering) or the under-standing of the social nuances of communication (nonverbal cues, use of humor). The diagnosis of Specific learning disorder is reserved for cases in which deficits are relegated to one or more areas of academic functioning (reading, writing, mathematic), and are not reflective of a global deficit in overall cognitive abilities.

Finally, the differential diagnosis of autism spectrum disorder is difficult, as individuals on the autism spectrum demonstrate deficits in adaptive functioning. These deficits, however, are not attributed to lower than average intelligence, but rather are better accounted for by social-communication difficulties and rigidity of behavior. The authors of the DSM-5 give caution when assessing individuals with suspected autism spectrum disorder and intellectual disability, as assessment of the communication difficulties observed in both disorders can be uniquely challenging. Clinicians should use their judgment when selecting instruments to assess intellectual functioning with individuals with pronounced communication difficulties.

CHAPTER 3

Evaluation and Assessment of Individuals with Intellectual Disability

This chapter provides an overview of assessments that have been demonstrated to be reliable and valid in the evaluation and assessment of intellectual disability. Generalized assessments of intellectual and adaptive functioning are outlined. Central to the diagnostic features of intellectual disability in the *Diagnostic and Statistical Manual of Mental Disorders* (DSM-5) is the requirement that the onset of intellectual and adaptive deficits occur during the developmental period. Additionally, earlier identification and intervention of intellectual disability are associated with more positive outcomes (Ramey and Ramey 1998). For these reasons, greater focus is placed on assessment of children, though it is recognized that assessment of adults for intellectual disability is often necessary, such as in forensic applications or for individuals with intellectual disability undergoing evaluation to determine eligibility for financial assistance.

International Statistical Classification of Diseases and Related Health Problems-10

International Statistical Classification of Diseases and Related Health Problems (ICD-10) diagnoses for intellectual disability are generally similar to those of DSM-5 although different codes are employed. Mild intellectual disability (code F70) generally represents intelligence quotients (IQ) of 50 to 70. Moderate intellectual disability (code F71) generally represents IQ of 35 to 49. Severe intellectual disability (code F72) represents IQ of 20 to 34. Profound intellectual disability (code 73) represents IQ below 20. There are two additional, poorly defined and rarely used codes for intellectual disability represented by F78 (Other intellectual disability) and F79 (Unspecified Intellectual Disability).

Essential to a comprehensive evaluation of individuals with intellectual disability is the assessment of intellectual functioning and adaptive behavior. Intellectual functioning is typically assessed through the use of standardized IQ tests, such as the Wechsler Intelligence Scales and Stanford–Binet Intelligence Scales. These measures provide profiles of functioning in several cognitive domains such as reasoning, problem solving, and abstract thinking. Measures of adaptive functioning, such as the Adaptive Behavior Assessment System-II (ABAS-II; Harrison and Oakland 2003) or Vineland Adaptive Behavior Scales-II (Vineland-II; Sparrow, Cicchetti, and Balla 2005), are used to assess an individual's capacity for engaging in the tasks of daily living and social independence. These two functional domains are the main aspects of clinical focus in the assessment of intellectual disability. The American Association of Intellectual and Developmental Disabilities (AAIDD) provides a framework for the assessment of individuals with intellectual disability, which the reader may find useful (Schalock et al. 2010). The third diagnostic consideration in the assessment of intellectual disability is the age of onset. As intellectual disability is a neurodevelopmental disorder, the DSM-5 specifies that the onset must occur during the developmental period, which means that symptoms develop during childhood or adolescence (American Psychological Association [APA] 2013).

There are several characteristics of standardized tests that the clinician should be familiar with. First, standardized tests are based on normative groups. It is the comparison of an individual's scores to the normative group that makes them interpretable. Thus, it is vital to assessment validity that the clinician choose an appropriate normative group for comparison. Standardized scores create a normal distribution, or bell curve, in which the vast majority of scores will fall within two standard deviations of the mean. On a measure with a mean of 100 and a standard deviation of 15, approximately 68 percent of scores will fall between 85 and 115 and 95 percent of scores will fall between 70 and 130. When assessing individuals with intellectual disability, the clinician is generally interested in whether or not, or the extent to which, scores exceed two standard deviations below the mean. It is important to remember that all standardized tests come with some degree of measurement error; thus, the clinician should consider the confidence interval when making decisions based on standardized test scores. For instance, the 95 percent confidence interval for a score of 70 on the Wechsler Adult Intelligence Scale-Fourth Edition (WAIS-IV) is ±5 points. Thus, the clinician can say with 95 percent certainty that the true score falls somewhere between 65 and 75.

In selection of the appropriate test, the American Psychological Association Task Force on Test User Qualifications recommends that individuals have sufficient knowledge of the intended use of the test score, knowledge of the procedures used during test development (which includes the constructs measured, the context of intended use, evidence of validity, and administration procedures), any characteristics of the test takers that affect the validity of interpretation, and test limitations (APA 2000). Test users should be aware of the qualifications required for the administration and interpretation of any psychological measures employed in the assessment process, as well as any legal and ethical issues specific to the population of interest. Measures used to assess intellectual and adaptive functioning should be culturally appropriate and psychometrically sound. Decisions concerning diagnosis, classification, and intervention should be based on a comprehensive evaluation consisting of multiple methods of assessment.

American Association of Intellectual and Developmental Disabilities Framework for Assessment of Intellectual Disability

In its 2010 manual, the AAIDD presented a framework for assessing individuals with intellectual disability that includes three assessment functions on which decisions and recommendations should be based: diagnosis, classification, and planning individualized systems of support. The clinician should be mindful of the purpose that each assessment strategy is meant to serve. Each assessment function should meet the following three criteria: instruments employed are appropriate for the purpose of the assessment, assessment data are valid, and results have useful application beneficial to the individual (Schalock et al. 2010).

There are numerous reasons why individuals with intellectual disability may need to be classified, such as need for supports, research purposes, and reimbursement or funding. Classification can be based on intellectual function, adaptive behavior, or need for supports. It is important that the assessment methods employed for classification be consistent with the specific purpose of classification. For instance, classification by IQ level is appropriate for research purposes, but not necessarily appropriate for making decisions about residential and educational placements. Classification systems should be beneficial to every person in the group. A common function of assessment is the identification of individuals eligible to receive special services and benefits. In the 36th Annual U.S. Department of Education Report to Congress on the Implementation of the Individuals with Disabilities Education Act (IDEA), students aged 6 to 21 years classified as having intellectual disability comprised 7.3 percent of the 5,823,844 served by IDEA in 2012 (U.S. Department of Education, 2014). Planning and developing individualized support systems should involve information from a variety of assessment sources, such as knowledgeable informants and formal and informal assessments, and be focused on improving specific outcomes (Schalock et al. 2010).

Generalized Assessments

Measures of Intelligence

Criterion A of the of the DSM-5 for intellectual disability requires that the individual demonstrate "deficits in intellectual functions, such as reasoning, problem solving, planning, abstract thinking, judgment, academic learning, and learning from experience, confirmed by both clinical assessment and individualized, standardized intelligence testing" (APA 2013). The generalized cognitive deficits outlined in Criterion A are typically assessed through the use of IQ tests, such as the Wechsler Intelligence Scales. In the DSM-IV-TR, individuals scoring approximately two standard deviations or more below the standardized population mean were considered to be in the Intellectually Disabled range. In the DSM-5, greater diagnostic emphasis was placed on adaptive functioning rather than IQ scores. These recommendations were relaxed somewhat in the DSM-5 to include a margin of measurement error, such that on a test with a mean of 100 and a standard deviation of 15, individuals scoring between 65 and 75 may or may not be appropriate for a diagnosis of intellectual disability depending on their level of adaptive functioning.

The DSM-5 describes the intellectual functions of interest as those involving reasoning, problem solving, planning, abstract thinking, judgment, learning from instruction and experience, and practical understanding. It goes on to mention verbal comprehension, working memory, perceptual reasoning, quantitative reasoning, abstract thought, and cognitive efficacy (APA 2013). The intelligence measures outlined in the following are useful assessments for these critical domains.

The AAIDD recommends use of the Wechsler Intelligence Scales or Stanford–Binet Intelligence Scales for use in the assessment of individuals with intellectual disability and that assessments used are individually administered and based on standardized norms (Schalock et al. 2010). The Wechsler Intelligence Scales, including the WAIS-IV and Wechsler Intelligence Scale for Children—Fifth Edition (WISC-V), are outlined as follows. Additionally, the Universal Nonverbal Intelligence Test (UNIT), a measure of intelligence that is administered completely nonverbally, is also described.

Verbal Intelligence Assessments

Wechsler Intelligence Scale for Children—Fifth Edition

As of 2016, the WISC-V is the latest Wechsler intelligence scale to be published (Wechsler 2014). In addition to the full-scale IQ (FSIQ) derived from seven subtest scaled scores, the WISC-V provides a total 13 index scores if the full battery is administered. The five primary index scaled scores are composed of the Verbal Comprehension Index (VCI), Visual Spatial Index (VSI), Fluid Reasoning Index (FRI), Working Memory Index (WMI), and Processing Speed Index (PSI). Each primary index score is a composite of two of the ten primary subtests. Descriptive classifications range from *Extremely Low* (≤69) to *Very Superior* (≥130).

Administration

The WISC-V should be administered individually in a quiet room that is free of distractions. The full battery should be administered in one session. All primary subtests must be administered to derive the FSIQ; however, one supplementary subtest within the corresponding index may be substituted for an invalid primary subtest or if the child is unable to properly complete a primary subtest due to a physical condition.

Interpretation

WISC-V profile interpretation begins with performing the profile analysis. First, report the FSIQ score as well as the corresponding percentile rank and confidence interval. Next, report and describe the VCI, VSI, FRI, WMI, and PSI. Critical values for statistically significant differences in index scores are provided for comparisons at the index level. Additionally, base rates for index-level discrepancies are provided to evaluate the relative rarity of a discrepancy. Index-level comparisons can provide insight into an individual's relative strengths and weaknesses in the corresponding cognitive domains. For example, a statistically significant elevation in VCI scores in comparison to FRI scores may suggest a relative strength in crystallized abilities over fluid reasoning abilities. Examination at this level should be guided by an a priori rationale. Finally, subtest-level comparisons may inform index-level interpretations. Evaluation of strengths and weaknesses at the subtest level should also be guided by an a priori rationale and not used to confirm or disconfirm a diagnosis.

Standardization

The WISC-V standardization sample consisted of 2,200 participants aged 6 to 16 years divided into 13 age groups and stratified according to age, sex, race or ethnicity, education level, and geographic region according to 2012 U.S. Census data. Data were also collected from 13 special groups, including individuals with mild or moderate intellectual disability. The mean FSIQ for the mild intellectual disability sample was 60.9, with primary index scores ranging from 65.1 for the WMI to 71.6 for the PSI. Of the FSIQ scores in the mild intellectual disability sample, 96 percent fell at or below 75. For the moderate intellectual disability sample, the mean FSIQ was 49.7 with primary index scores ranging from 55.2 on the VCI to 59.3 on the PSI. For comparison, only 5 percent of children in the control group FSIQ scores fell at or below 75 and no children in the control group obtained FSIQ scores of 60 or lower.

Limitations

The WISC-V is not intended to diagnose disorders, and scores should be considered in the context of a comprehensive clinical assessment and not be interpreted in isolation.

Wechsler Adult Intelligence Scale—Fourth Edition

The WAIS-IV was designed to measure cognitive functioning in individuals aged 16 to 90 years (Wechsler, Coalson, and Raiford 2008). It provides a FSIQ score representative of general intellectual functioning that is composed of four index scores: VCI, Perceptual Reasoning Index (PRI), WMI, and PSI. The core assessment consists of 10 subtests. Descriptive classifications range from *Extremely Low* (≤69) to *Very Superior* (≥130).

Administration

Administration of the WAIS-IV requires the use of the WAIS-IV testing materials, which include an administration manual, testing protocols, stimulus books, and a set of blocks. The WAIS-IV should be administered individually by a qualified test user in an environment free from distractions.

Interpretation

WAIS-IV profile interpretation begins with reporting the FSIQ score as well as the corresponding percentile rank and confidence interval. Next, report and describe the VCI, PRI, WMI, and PSI. The critical values for statistically significant differences in index scores are provided for comparisons at the index level. Additionally, base rates for index-level discrepancies are provided to evaluate the relative rarity of a discrepancy.

Index-level comparisons can provide insight into an individual's relative strengths and weaknesses. Finally, subtest-level comparisons may inform index-level interpretations.

Standardization

The WAIS-IV standardization sample consisted of 2,200 participants aged 16 to 90 years divided into 13 age groups and stratified according to age, sex, race or ethnicity, education level, and geographic region according to U.S. Census data from October 2005. Data were also collected from 13 special groups, including individuals with mild or moderate intellectual disability. Individuals with mild and moderate intellectual disability scored significantly lower than a matched control group, demonstrating mean composite scores that ranged from 58.5 FSIQ to 65.9 VCI. The cognitive profile for individuals with intellectual disability showed less variability among subtest and composite scores than samples from the general population. All (100 percent) of the individuals with mild intellectual disability obtained FSIQ scores less than or equal to 75, and 97 percent of individuals with moderate intellectual disability obtained FSIQ scores less than or equal to 60. For comparison, only seven percent of participants in the control group obtained FSIQ scores of 75 or less and three percent obtained FSIQ scores of 60 or less.

Limitations

WAIS-IV scores may provide evidence for or against a diagnosis of intellectual disability and may inform intervention and support planning in the context of a comprehensive evaluation; however, WAIS-IV scores alone are not sufficient for a diagnosis of intellectual disability.

Nonverbal Intelligence Assessment

Universal Nonverbal Intelligence Test

In cases in which individuals with intellectual disability have limited or no verbal ability, the use of nonverbal assessments may be appropriate (UNIT; Bracken and McCallum 1998). Evidence exists that use of nonverbal tests with individuals with intellectual disability may result in greater FSIQ scores than measures that rely on verbal language for administration (Thorndike, Hagen, and Sattler 1986).

The UNIT was designed to measure general intelligence and cognitive abilities in children and adolescents aged 5 to 17 years who may be disadvantaged by other measures of cognitive ability that are reliant on verbal expression and comprehension, which makes the UNIT particularly useful for children and adolescents with intellectual disability whose language abilities are diminished. Unlike most measures of intelligence, the UNIT is administered without the use of verbal instruction. This feature reduces the influence of culture on test scores and generally reduces between-group differences often found on verbal measures of intelligence. Abilities in memory, reasoning, symbolic, and nonsymbolic domains are measured. Additionally, a FSIQ and four index standard scores with a mean of 100 and a standard deviation of 15 are provided. Intellectual functioning is rated from *Very Delayed* to *Very Superior.*

The conceptual model of the UNIT utilizes six subtests (Symbolic Memory, Object Memory, Spatial Memory, Analogic Reasoning, Cube Design, and Mazes), which form the four scales. The Memory Quotient (MQ) is a measure of an individual's memory for content, location, and sequence. It is composed of the Symbolic Memory, Object Memory, and Spatial Memory subtests. The Reasoning Quotient (RQ) measures problem-solving ability in familiar and unfamiliar situations. Additionally, it measures planning, the ability to process patterns, and the ability to understand relationships such as those in geometric analogies. The RQ is composed of the Analogic Reasoning, Cube Design, and Mazes subtests. The Symbolic Quotient (SQ) measures the ability to solve problems which require the test taker to label, categorize, and organize meaningful symbols. The SQ is composed of the Symbolic Memory, Object Memory, and Analogic Reasoning subtests. Finally, the Nonsymbolic Quotient (NSQ) measures the ability to solve problems using abstract materials. The NSQ is composed of the Spatial Memory, Cube Design, and Mazes subtests.

Administration

The UNIT should be individually administered without the use of verbal directions in an environment in which the examinee feels secure.

Communication is limited to pantomime, gestures, and nonverbal demonstrations. Verbal communication not pertaining to the test or test procedures is permitted, such as those meant to provide encouragement. The gestures used in the administration of the UNIT include head nodding, head shaking, open-handed shrugging (indication that a response is required), pointing, hand waving, and giving a thumbs up.

Interpretation

Interpretation of UNIT performance follows three stages: FSIQ interpretation; MQ, RQ, SQ, and NSQ interpretation; and subtest interpretation. The FSIQ is interpreted both quantitatively and qualitatively. Quantitative interpretation consists of standard scores, confidence intervals, and percentile ranks, whereas, qualitative interpretation involves descriptive classifications such as *Very Superior* or *Very Delayed*. Second-stage interpretation involves examining the variability among index scores, which provides insights into the child's functioning and may inform planning for supports. For instance, if a child's NSQ score is significantly greater than his or her SQ score, it may be indicative of a language deficit. The learning environment may be enhanced by visual representations of the material presented. Similarly, performance variability may be examined at the subtest level in the third stage of interpretation. Individuals with intellectual disability are more likely to demonstrate a flat cognitive profile in relation to other groups, with slightly better perceptual organizational skills than verbal skills. Measures of abstract reasoning are especially difficult for this population.

Standardization

The standardization sample of the UNIT was composed of a representative sample of 2,100 children and adolescents proportionally stratified according to the U.S. population with respect to sex, race, Hispanic origin (Hispanic or non-Hispanic), region, community setting (urban or suburban, rural), classroom placement (full-time regular classroom, full-time self-contained classroom, part-time special education resource, and others), special education services (learning disability, speech and language impairments, serious emotional disturbance, mental retardation, giftedness, English as a second language and bilingual education, and regular education), and parental education attainment (less than high school degree, high school graduate or equivalent, some college or technical school, or four or more years of college). Stratification was based on 1995 U.S. Census data. Individuals diagnosed with mental retardation represented 1.2 percent of the sample. Roughly equal numbers of females and males were included in each age group.

The UNIT has been validated for use with children with intellectual disability, particularly in the mild to moderate ranges. A sample of 84 participants diagnosed with mental retardation according to the criteria set forth by DSM-IV or the American Association of Mental Retardation was utilized. Using a cutoff score of 70, the standard battery of the UNIT identified individuals diagnosed with mental retardation with an accuracy of 82.1 percent. The extended battery demonstrated an accuracy of 86.9 percent.

Limitations

The UNIT is only valid for use with children and adolescents aged 5 to 17 years. While many cultural and linguistic barriers are removed by nonverbal tests, the clinician should not assume that the UNIT is valid for use with all groups.

Test of Nonverbal Intelligence—Fourth Edition

The Test of Nonverbal Intelligence—Fourth Edition (TONI-4) is an individual assessment of general intelligence (TONI-4; Brown, Sherbenou, and Johnsen 2010). The TONI-4 is a brief measure, as it takes approximately 15 minutes to administer. The TONI-4 is able to assess intelligence in children and adolescents who have difficulty with language or motor skills. These deficits may confound results in other assessments of cognitive ability that are more verbal in nature. The test has both verbal and nonverbal instructions as well as instructions in several foreign languages. The TONI-4 utilizes figural problem-solving subtests and subtests for abstract reasoning to estimate general intelligence.

The TONI-4, an assessment of general intelligence for those who have hearing, language, or motor impairment, was designed to be used with children and adults. The ages range from 6 to 89 years. This assessment is utilized not only for estimating general intelligence, but also for identifying intellectual impairment, ruling out intellectual concerns in those who have language or motor impairments, and for formulating future interventions. The format of the TONI-4 consists of an untimed approach where the examiner must choose between oral and nonverbal directions. Nonverbal instructions are uniform to maintain a proficient estimate of cognitive ability without the possibility of confounding results. The nonverbal instructions advise the examiner to point at an empty box within the utilized Picture Book. The examiner then shifts the examinee's focus to the first response choice and shake his or her head for "no" or "yes" across the different possible choices to have the examinee understand how to make an appropriate response. When there appears to be a clear understanding of the process by the examinee, he or she is asked to complete training items and then the full task.

The TONI-4 is another useful test to account for intelligence and potential learning disabilities through the utilization of a nonverbal approach. The TONI-4 in itself cannot diagnose but is another component that can be utilized to obtain a fair score of intelligence. It can determine if there are prior language deficits, developmental aphasia, hearing impairment or deafness, and speech or motor deficits. The TONI-4 also does not utilize cultural symbols or pictures, which may benefit in the testing of those with different language and cultural backgrounds. The current normative sample for the TONI-4, however, is based on English speakers, with 77 percent given the assessment utilizing the English oral instructions and only 23 percent using the nonverbal instructions. This should be taken into account with future iterations and research on the TONI. The TONI-4 is thought to be valid and reliable for assessment of children, adolescents, and adults.

Leiter International Performance Scale—Third Edition

The Leiter-3 is an individual assessment of cognitive functioning in individuals from the ages of 3 to 75+ years (Leiter-3; Roid, Miller, and

Koch 2013). The Leiter-3 has measures of nonverbal intelligence through the assessment of fluid reasoning and visualization. The scale also measures nonverbal intelligence through assessment of nonverbal memory, attention, and cognitive interference. It was developed as a measure of cognitive functioning for groups of individuals consisting of those with significant communication disorders, autism, cognitive delay, learning disabilities, motor impairment, traumatic brain injury, hearing impairments, and for those whose first language is not English. The Leiter-3 includes nonverbal instructions where the examiner pantomimes to the examinee. This consists of head and hand movements and facial expressions within the demonstration so that the examinee understands the nature of the subtest. The examiner initially gets the examinees attention through the use of focused eye contact and hand signals. The Leiter-3 consists of 10 subtests that are distributed into two groups. All subtests have a restart rule where, if the examinee cannot get the correct answer at start, even after teaching, the examiner will then proceed with the preceding age group starting point. The cognitive battery group consists of five subtests: Classification or Analogies, Sequential Order, Figure Ground, Form Completion, and Visual Patterns. The Leiter-3 has an Attention or Memory Battery that consists of two memory subtests, two nonverbal attention subtests, and the Stroop subtest.

Peabody Picture Vocabulary Test—Fourth Edition

The Peabody Picture Vocabulary Test—Fourth Edition (PPVT-4) is a measure of receptive vocabulary in children, adolescents, and adults (PPVT-4; Dunn and Dunn 2007). In the PPVT-4, the examinee is shown four colored pictures arranged on a page and is then asked to select the picture that best fits the meaning of a stimulus word said by the examiner. The PPVT-4 does not require expressive language but rather is an evaluation of the examinee's comprehension of acquired vocabulary. The test is useful among nonreaders and individuals with written language difficulties, as it requires no reading or writing. The PPVT-4 is an untimed test of vocabulary and is useful as a nonverbal assessment in testing hearing vocabulary, as examinees are not required to say their answer.

Wechsler Nonverbal Scale of Ability

The Wechsler Nonverbal Scale of Ability (WNV) was designed for individuals with language disorders, who are deaf or hard of hearing, and who do not speak English (WNV; Wechsler 2006). The WNV tried to provide a fair assessment of knowledge for individuals belonging to one of these groups. The WNV was made as a modification to the original Wechsler Scales as seen in the WISC and WAIS. The WNV expanded these assessments to those with language constraints, as it gives these examinees a fair look at their intellectual ability. The WNV has six subtests: Matrixes Coding, Object Assembly, Recognition, Spatial Span, and Picture Arrangement.

Tests of Adaptive Functioning

Criterion B for intellectual disability in the DSM-5 requires that an individual display deficits "in adaptive functioning that result in failure to meet developmental and sociocultural standards for personal independence and social responsibility. Without ongoing support, the adaptive deficits limit functioning in one or more activities of daily life, such as communication, social participation, and independent living, across multiple environments, such as home, school, work, and community" (APA 2013, 33).

A major change in the DSM-5 from the DSM-IV-TR involved classifying the severity of intellectual disability by levels of adaptive functioning rather than prescribed ranges of IQ scores. In the DSM-IV-TR, the severity of intellectual disability (then classified as mental retardation) was determined by the IQ score. The DSM-5 conceptualizes the severity of intellectual disability across three broad domains of adaptive functioning: conceptual, social, and practical. The areas of interest in the conceptual domain are of an academic nature, outlined in the DSM-5 as competence in memory, language, reading, writing, math reasoning, acquisition of practical knowledge, problem solving, and judgment in novel situations. The social domain involves empathy, communication, and awareness of the thoughts and feelings of others. The practical domain involves self-care, learning, and the ability to apply what has been learned across settings such as work and school (APA 2013).

Often it is necessary to involve third parties in the assessment process of individuals with intellectual disability. Measures of adaptive functioning often involve ratings from parents, teachers, and other caregivers familiar with the daily functioning of the individual to supplement the clinical assessment. The AAIDD recommends that clinicians employ standardized measures based on general population norms in the assessment of adaptive functioning (Schalock et al. 2010).

Adaptive Behavior Rating Scale-Second Edition

The ABAS-II is a measure of adaptive behavior designed to aid in diagnostic assessment, identification of strengths and limitations, and intervention planning for individuals from birth to 89 years of age (Harrison and Oakland 2003). Administration includes five rating forms, which are completed by a variety of respondents familiar with the individual being assessed, such as teachers, caregivers, parents, and family members. Additionally, an adult form is provided, which can be completed by the individual being assessed (aged 16 to 89 years). The ABAS-II provides skill area scaled scores for the conceptual, social, and practical domains of adaptive functioning consistent with the DSM-5 as well as a General Adaptive Composite (GAC) score that serves as a global measure of functioning. The descriptive classifications for GAC scores range from *Extremely Low* to *Very Superior*. Skill area scaled scores are derived from seven, nine, or ten skill area ratings depending on the age of the examinee. Skill areas include communication, community use, functional academics, home living, health and safety, leisure, self-care, self-direction, and social measures.

Administration

Administration of the ABAS-II requires the rating form, a pencil, and an environment free of distractions. Examiners should establish rapport with respondents prior to administration. The ABAS-II rating forms should be administered to multiple carefully selected respondents whenever possible to improve assessment validity. Respondents should have frequent and recent contact with the individual for several hours at a time, and have had the opportunity to observe the skills measured by the ABAS-II.

Respondents should be informed of the purpose of the assessment and the required expectations of sufficient familiarity with the individual being assessed as well as honesty and objectivity. In general, items can be understood by individuals with a sixth-grade reading level.

Interpretation

Prior to interpretation, the test user should review the accuracy of the data, resolve conflicting data, and consider the effects of respondent guessing. The test user should first examine the GAC score to compare the examinee's global level adaptive functioning to normative age groups. The GAC has a mean score of 100 and a standard deviation of 15, with individuals scoring 70 or below falling into the *Extremely Low* classification. The skill area scaled scores are then examined to identify areas of relative strengths and weaknesses among the conceptual, social, and practical domains. Finally, variability among scores in specific skill areas may be examined.

Standardization

The standardization samples for the ABAS-II varied by rating form. All were based on U.S. Census data and were representative of the U.S. English-speaking population. Standardization samples were stratified according to sex, race or ethnicity, and education level.

Limitations

Interpretations of ABAS-II scores should consider that ratings are subject to the bias of respondents. The clinician should carefully follow the interpretation guidelines for ensuring that data are as accurate as possible.

Achievement Tests

Achievement tests are not required for the diagnosis of intellectual disability, but comprehensive tests are useful in seeing the impact of the intellectual issues on the individuals' academic performance. As noted in the first chapter, the presentation of individuals with the same IQ may differ greatly and this additional information may add important insights even if it does not affect the diagnosis per se.

The Wide Range Achievement Test—Fourth Edition

This is a relatively brief assessment that measures skills such as word-reading ability, spelling, reading comprehension, and arithmetic (Wide Range Achievement Test—Fourth Edition [WRAT-4]; Wilkinson and Robertson 2006). This norm-referenced test is available in alternate forms, which allows for serial testing without the concern of practice effects, and has norms available for clients aged 5 to 94 years.

The WRAT-4 is an excellent, brief measure that is useful in estimating premorbid intellectual functioning, writing ability, basic math skills, and comprehension. It may prove useful as a screening measure to help guide additional, more specific tests of achievement. While the WRAT-4 is helpful, it does not evaluate the client on knowledge of words and comprehension of complex and lengthy narratives, which could prompt the clinician to use other measures that assess such abilities.

Woodcock–Johnson Tests of Achievement—Fourth Edition

One of the most widely used measures when evaluating learning disorders is the Woodcock–Johnson Tests of Achievement (e.g., this test is required in nearly all academic evaluations in Florida schools) (WJ-Ach 4; Shrank, Mather, and McGrew 2014). This instrument is frequently used in conjunction with the Woodcock–Johnson Tests of Cognitive Abilities (WJ-Cog) and Woodcock–Johnson Tests of Oral Language (WJ-OL), which can help us to identify strengths and weaknesses in terms of language abilities along with intellectual skills. The WJ-Ach 4 is the incorporation of subtests that tap into broad achievement areas that can help with conceptualization of different types of learning strengths and weaknesses. Scoring for all forms of the Woodcock–Johnson requires the clinician to tally a total score for the individual subtest and enter the scores in a computerized scoring system.

Key Math-3 Diagnostic Assessment

The Key Math-3 Diagnostic Assessment (KM-3 DA) is a helpful tool when there is a concern of a possible mathematics disorder (KM-3 DA; Connolly 2007). The core constructs assessed by the KM-3 DA revolve around three components including knowledge and understanding of basic and complex mathematical principles, ability to perform computational tasks, and applying such knowledge to solve advanced mathematical problems (Connolly 2007). The KM-3 DA consists of 10 subtests that assess a wide variety of basic and complex math skills. These subtests include Numeration, Algebra, Geometry, Measurement, Data Analysis and Probability, Mental Computation and Estimation, Addition and Subtraction, Multiplication and Division, Foundations of Problem Solving, and Applied Problem Solving.

Other Tests

As noted earlier, no additional tests are required to diagnose an intellectual disability, but other tests can be used effectively to further detail the nature of the client's problems beyond that yielded by the required IQ and adaptive function tests. These tests sometimes yield surprising results in terms of strengths, which are not expected based on overall functioning. This is most often seen in those with mild mental disabilities with IQs that exceed 50. These tests can include measures of memory (e.g., Wechsler Memory Scale [WMS-IV; Wechsler, 2009]: Wide Range Assessment and Language [WRAML-2; Sheslow and Adams 2003]; California Verbal Learning Test [Delis et al. 1994]); aphasia (e.g., Boston Diagnostic Aphasia Examination [Kaplan 1983]; Boston Naming Test [Kaplan, Goodglass and Weintraub 2001]); executive function (e.g., Delis-Kaplan Executive Function System [D-KEFS; Delis, Kaplan and Kramer 2001]; Figural Fluency Test [Ruff 1996]; Halstead Category Test-Revised [Russell and Levy 1987]; Wisconsin card Sort Test [WCST; Heaton 1993]; DSS Rey Osterrieth Complex Figure Test [Bernstein and Waber 1996]; Tower of London [TOWL: Hammill and Larsen 2009]; Stroop Color and Word Test [STROOP; Golden 1978]; Conner's Performance Test [Conners, Staff 2000]; VST such as the Hooper Visual Organization Test [Hooper 1983] and the Bender-Gestalt [Hutt 1963]); and motor and sensory tests (Finger Tapping Test [FTT; Reitan 1985]; Purdue Pegboard [Tiffin 1968]; Grooved Pegboard [Trites 1989]). This list is by no means exhaustive; any test can be used if the client is able to follow the directions and understand what is required.

Concluding Remarks

This chapter provides a brief overview of current measures of intelligence and adaptive functioning that have been validated for use with individuals with intellectual disabilities; however, it is by no means exhaustive. The reader is encouraged to become familiar with a variety of assessment instruments in order to better serve the intellectual disability population. In addition to measuring intellectual and adaptive functioning, it may also be useful to supplement assessment with measures of achievement, such as the Woodcock–Johnson measures or the WRAT-4, to better assess academic achievement. Finally, the elevated incidence of motor and sensory deficits among individuals with intellectual disability and the complexities of comorbidity are important areas to consider when working with this population (Carvill 2001). The following chapter examines assessments that may be appropriate for use for individuals with comorbid sensory and motor disabilities.

Assessment of Persons with Intellectual Disabilities and Sensory Impairments

Among children with recognized disabilities in 2011, less than 2 percent consisted of children with sensory impairment and comprised 0.2 percent of all school-age children in the United States (National Center on Education Statistics [NCES] 2012). The prevalence of sensory impairments is significantly higher among individuals with intellectual disability as compared to the general population and psychiatric samples (Carvill 2001; Wilson and Haire 1990). The presence of sensory impairment introduces several critical issues to be addressed by the examiner when assessing intelligence or other cognitive functioning. The examiner must carefully consider the purpose of the assessment (to measure intelligence, or to quantify the degree of sensory impairment), the selection of tests appropriate for the individual, and consider whether to administer the test using standardized procedures, or provide some level of accommodations to compensate for sensory impairment. Finally, the examiner must be able to interpret the results to provide the family or referral source with an accurate estimate of intelligence, cognitive functioning, capacity for learning, and functioning in the real world. This chapter provides an overview of some issues related to the assessment of individuals with intellectual disability and auditory, visual-perceptual, and motor impairments. In the following section on hearing impairments, we review Wilhoit and McCallum's (2003) method of cross-battery assessment for estimating intelligence in the hearing impaired. Although the method was specifically developed with reference to hearing-impaired populations, the process of assessment described by the authors may be helpful to provide a theoretically derived and evidence-based structure to the assessment of individuals for whom valid and reliable measures of intelligence may not be appropriately developed for specific types and combinations of sensory-motor deficits.

A general issue in the assessment in intellectual disabilities is that appropriate reference groups (e.g., with seeing, hearing, or other sensory impairment) are often lacking in the standardization samples of many popular intelligence tests. This issue is particularly pronounced when additional sensory motor issues are present. The American Association on Intellectual and Developmental Disabilities (AAIDD 2010) states that tests such as the Wechsler Scales or Stanford–Binet Intelligence Scales are preferable as estimates of intelligence because they capture a broad range of abilities that are highly correlated to behavior and other cognitive measures. The aforementioned tests are guided by the widely accepted theory of general intelligence or g hypothesized by Cattell, Horn, and Carroll (McGrew and Flanagan 1998). However, the official position of the AAIDD states that these tests may not be appropriate for some individuals with sensory impairments and profound intellectual disability. Crisp (2007) and others have warned against the inappropriate application of an intellectual disability diagnosis to an individual whose true intellectual abilities are underestimated by conventional intellectual assessments.

Instead, AAIDD recommends alternative tests, such as the Comprehensive C-TONI (Hammill, Pearson, and Wiederholt 1997) for individuals who are mute, or the Slosson Intelligence Test–Revised (Slosson,

Nicholson, and Hibpshman 1991) for cases of profound impairment. The AAIDD does not clearly recommend or suggest "best tests" or "best practices" regarding intellectual assessment of individuals with intellectual and sensory impairments, largely because research and available tests with appropriate reference groups are quite limited. Given these ambiguities, professional consensus indicates that clinicians are to use extreme caution in the assessment of intellectual disability when the individual is impaired in visual, auditory, or motor functioning.

Sansone et al. (2014) recommended that when clinicians are interpreting the scores from standardized test batteries, standard scores should not be used. The authors found that among 103 children with fragile X syndrome (the leading congenital cause of intellectual disability), variability in scores was improved when raw scores were converted to z-scores using the data from the standardization sample, rather than converting raw scores to standardized scores. When children are tested on measures for which they do not fit the normative sample, the z-transformation approach may be a more accurate way to examine intelligence at the extreme low end of the normal distribution of scores.

Estimates of intellectual functioning are often "overshadowed" by the sensory impairment, since impairments in vision or hearing early in life typically reduce opportunities for learning and typical developmental processes. The functional impact of visual impairment or blindness is thought to cause more severe impairment than auditory impairment. For example, blind individuals with intellectual disability are more likely to have motor impairments than hearing impaired intellectually disabled persons. Children with congenital or acquired deafness and low intellectual functioning may fail to develop systems of communication with others due to inadequate experiences during critical developmental periods. Individuals may have impairment across multiple modalities. It is critical that the clinician does not penalize the individuals' intelligence for their sensory-motor impairments, though it may be difficult to disentangle sensory functioning from cognitive functioning.

While there exists a growing literature on the topic of assessing children with multiple physical, cognitive, and sensory impairments, there are relatively few published norms standardized with these specialty populations to compare an individual's respondent's scores with. Norm-referenced scores are typically normally distributed and most suitable for individuals who fall into the middle ranges of the distribution. Such tests are more likely to be insensitive to scores of individuals who fall into the extreme ends of intelligence due to floor and ceiling effects inherent in the tests. Furthermore, the assessment of sensory-motor functioning is not highly predictive of cognitive functioning in children younger than two years, at which time estimates of intelligence become more reliable (Vig and Sanders 2007). In infants, the Bayley Scales of Infant Development (Bayley 1993) and the Griffiths Mental Development Scales (Griffiths 1976; Huntley 1996) measure progress in developmental skills. Skills are assessed largely within sensory-motor domains, and scores yield "mental age equivalents" as an alternative measure of intelligence for the very young. The Bayley scales are moderately correlated (.70) to the Wechsler Preschool and Primary Scales of Intelligence (WPPSI; Wechsler 2012), and have a very low scoring floor.

In some cases, it may be appropriate to grant an individual accommodations during testing. Accommodations do not change the concepts being measured on the test. Examples include administering the test in braille, large print, or audio formats, allowing for mute respondents to make responses through eye gaze or using gestures, sign language, or communication boards, and tactile communication devices; for example, test modifications, on the other hand, do change the constructs being tested (e.g., using a memory aid or calculator in a memory or achievement test), and are generally not appropriate for the purposes of assessment. Testing accommodations may invalidate the standardized administration procedures. The use of accommodations prevents the clinician from discerning whether poor test performance, as compared to individuals in the test's standardization sample, reflects actual ability, or mere differences in administration procedures. When standard administration procedures cannot be used and use of accommodations is necessary, only those accommodations that have been tested empirically to determine that they do not threaten test validity are to be used. For example, Braden and Elliot (2003) have provided explicit guidelines on the use of acceptable and unacceptable accommodations for sensory impairment when using the Stanford–Binet Intelligence Scale (Fifth Edition). Sattler (2008) and Sattler and Ryan (2009) have provided similar guidelines for assessing individuals with sensory impairment using the Wechsler Intelligence Scales for Children (Fourth Edition) and Wechsler Adult Intelligence Scales (Fourth Edition), respectively. Finally, interpretations of tests in which accommodations are used should be made with caution, and with consultation of a clinician who has expertise in the sensory impairment, if possible.

If a stand-alone test is not available to use with a particular individual, a cautious application of a cross-battery assessment may represent the best alternative to assessing intellectual function. A cross-battery approach is based on the tenants of the Cattell–Horn–Carroll (CHC) theory of intelligence. This theory states that intelligence represents a person's ability in broad cognitive domains, and the intelligence assessment should strive to capture a wide range of the broader cognitive domain; each broad domain should be assessed using at least two narrow and qualitatively distinct measures of the domain-construct. Broad domains in CHC theory include Crystallized Intelligence (Gc), Fluid Intelligence (Gf), Quantitative Knowledge (Gq), Reading and Writing Ability (Grw), Short-Term Memory (Gsm), Visual Processing (Gv), Auditory Processing (Ga), Long-Term Storage and Retrieval (Glr), Processing Speed (Gs), and Decision or Reaction Time or Speed (Gt). CHC theory is widely supported by factor analysis and has provided both the theoretical and structural bases for many multidimensional tests of intelligence, including the Wechsler and Stanford–Binet intelligence scales, and Woodcock–Johnson cognitive batteries.

When the purpose of the assessment is to measure the degree of sensory impairment, then tests requiring the impaired modality must be administered. In this case, tests specifically designed to measure intelligence would generally not be appropriate for testing sensory impairment. When the goal is to measure intelligence, it is common practice for clinicians to simply omit the subtests from a measure requiring response in the modality that is impaired for the individual. If a person's intelligence is measured using a subtest that does require use of the impaired sensory modality, performance is less representative of intelligence and more indicative of the level of sensory impairment. However, test selection depends on the level of impairment. It is imperative to have the child's vision, hearing, health, and pain assessed before any instruments are given, and to determine whether the individual can read, write, and comprehend speech. The later skills can be examined informally by asking the individual to describe a picture, assemble a puzzle, read and write short sentences, and respond to questions.

Assessment of Adaptive Functioning

The assessment of adaptive functioning is a separate and critical part of the evaluation of intellectual disability. However, it is not appropriate to penalize an individual's intelligence based on his or her sensory or motor impairment; this is not the case with adaptive functioning. The goal of this assessment is to determine the person's level of independence with real-world tasks expected for their age level; therefore, assistance should not be given to the individual if asked to demonstrate performance ability. However, individuals are to be rated in accordance with any assistive *technology* they may use (e.g., hearing aid, glasses, wheelchair, etc.). The measures may underestimate the abilities of individuals who are blind or have visual impairment. A variety of norm- and criterion-referenced rating scales are available. Popular measures include the Scales of Independent Behavior–Revised (for ages infancy to 80+ years), Vineland Adaptive Behavior Scales—Second Edition (for ages birth to 90+ years), Adaptive Behavior Assessment System—Second Edition (for ages birth to 89 years), Diagnostic Adaptive Behavior Scale (for ages 4 to 21 years), the Adaptive Behavior Evaluation Scale–Revised (for ages 4 to 12 years), and the Brigance Inventory of Early Development—Third Edition (criterion-referenced and norm-referenced scoring versions).

Training and Experience

Most evaluators are not trained or experienced in evaluating individuals who have sensory impairments. Evaluators must incorporate the expertise and experience of visual impairment professionals and collaborate with them throughout the evaluation process, from preparation through report writing. Collaborative consultation with an audiologist, ophthalmologist, physician, or occupational therapist may be necessary to assess the degree of impairment. This should be completed before intellectual assessment in order to guide the selection of appropriate tests and their interpretation.

Guidelines for Report Writing

In many cases, testing the intelligence of children with intellectual disability and sensory impairments will require that some subtests are not administered, administration procedures may be accommodated or partially violated, or the tests may not be specifically normed for use with the appropriate population of interest. Given these barriers, it is important that the clinician clearly state the limitations of the assessment, including the extent to which scores may be a valid and reliable estimate of the individual's abilities. If adaptations to the test materials or administration procedures are used, they must be reported clearly and precisely. Score interpretation should acknowledge if the instruments have not been normed using individuals with the particular sensory impairment in question. Test scores should be reported using confidence intervals, at a confidence level of at least 90 percent (Goodman, Evans, and Loftin 2011).

Assessments for the Deaf

Legal definitions of deafness may vary by state and hold variable clinical meanings. Auditory acuity and the classification of hearing loss is based on the extent to which an individual requires greater than average intensity of sound (measured in decibels) to hear what a normally hearing individual could discern at lower volume. When testing intelligence in children with deafness or hearing loss, it is recommended that the clinician or interdisciplinary team first determine the parameters of hearing loss. In school-aged children, the most common type of hearing loss includes conductive hearing loss, whereby structural damage or mechanical restriction of the middle ear prevents sound transmission to neural structures. This may be caused by ear infections of other inflammatory conditions. A second type of hearing loss is that caused by damage to neural pathways in the ear or auditory cortex. Hearing loss may also involve mixed impairment in conductive and sensory-neural processes. Beyond the type and degree of hearing loss, other factors known to affect the potential for learning in children with hearing impairment include the time hearing loss occurred and was identified; whether early intervention services were received by the individual, their quality, and quantity; whether the individual uses adaptive technology (e.g., hearing aid, cochlear implant, communication board, frequency modulation system); the family's language at home (e.g., American Sign Language, spoken English, other language); family attitude toward hearing loss; presence of other disability or impairment, and cultural identity (Ferrell, Bruce, and Luckner 2014).

When testing an individual with hearing impairment, Sattler (2008) and Sattler and Ryan (2009) provide several recommendations. First, give credit for responses that are communicated in any modality. If the child appears to require assistance, ask the individual how you may help him or her. Always speak to the individual face to face. Many individuals with hearing impairment are sensitive to visual cues, particularly your facial expressions and gestures. Do not exaggerate lip movements when speaking. Consider whether your movements and expressions help you to communicate with the person or whether you may be a source of distraction during testing. When testing, be sure to smile to reward the person's effort, but do not make faces when the person answers correctly or incorrectly. If the individual uses hearing aids, ensure that they are turned on and functioning properly. Instructions may be delivered in pantomime, where appropriate.

Few intelligence tests have been designed and standardized specifically for use with deaf and hearing-impaired children. For this reason, intelligence is typically estimated by prorating scores from nonverbal subtests only from popular intelligence tests such as the WAIS or WISC series. This practice is supported by consistent research findings indicating that the distribution of nonverbal intelligence between hearing-impaired and nonhearing-impaired children is the same. These suggest that separate norms are not necessary for interpreting estimates of intelligence in children with hearing impairments. Administration of nonverbal measures should be conducted in the same fashion as for children without hearing impairment (Hill-Briggs et al. 2007).

Verbal intelligence tests assume that children are equally exposed to verbal information and knowledge. Hearing loss is strongly associated with reduced opportunity for acquiring verbal information, and therefore poor performance on verbal subtests in the hearing impaired may reflect aptitude or they may reflect differences in environmental factors. The use of verbal subtests is therefore not an acceptable estimate of general intelligence for deaf individuals (Braden 1994). However, Kamphaus (1993) cautions against simply dropping the verbal subtests from intelligence tests assessing both verbal and nonverbal abilities, by prorating the respondent's full-scale intelligence score, because it would be difficult for the clinician to determine whether poor performance would be reflective of intellectual ability or merely due to changes in administration procedures. Others (Kamphaus 1993; Wilhoit and McCallum 2003) recommend that when intelligence is prorated using nonverbal subtests from a test that measures both verbal and nonverbal abilities, the clinician should administer an additional intelligence test specific to nonverbal abilities to cross-validate the interpretations of the prorated test performance.

Wilhoit and McCallum (2003) describe a seven-step approach to the cross-battery assessment of nonverbal functions in individuals with hearing impairments, based on the CHC theory of intelligence (Flanagan and McGrew 1997; McGrew and Flanagan 1998). The following approach provides a useful framework for assessing cognitive function in the face of sensory or intellectual limitations, and may be useful for assessing children with intellectual disabilities and other sensory-motor impairments (e.g., visual impairment, motor deficits). The technique has also been criticized by Watkins, Youngstrom, and Glutting (2002) for its overreliance on clinical judgment and rational analysis, inherent error introduced by violating standardization procedures or administering subtests out of order, the possible inappropriate comparison of scores from different tests, and the possible inefficient use of time and expense required for assessment. Clearly, additional research and instruments for use with intellectually disabled individuals with hearing impairments are needed, but until more appropriate methods are available and tested, clinicians are faced with the challenge of using the best available techniques and methods with their patients.

1. *Selection of an appropriate test battery.* The test battery should be multidimensional and allow for an adequate coverage of Gf and Gc.

The examiner would want to avoid the selection of subtests from different test batteries so that the results of each subtest can be interpreted together. While the presence of sensory impairments may preclude reliance on multiple test batteries, clinicians must strive to use the fewest number of batteries to minimize the measurement error introduced by use of multiple standardization samples. When the assessment is conducted for the purpose of obtaining disability or educational placement services, clinicians must be aware of state-specific laws regarding acceptable measures for quantifying an FSIQ score (including prorating procedures). At the time of publication, Wilhoit and McCallum (2003) recommended use of the Leiter International Performance Scale (Roid, Miller, and Koch 2013) and the UNIT (Bracken and McCallum 1998).

2. *Determine that "crystallized intelligence" and "fluid reasoning" domains are properly represented by at least two subtests.* Clinicians are responsible for determining that the core test battery adequately represents both narrow and broad Gf and Gc abilities. For the interested reader, McGrew and Flanagan (1998) and Flanagan, Ortiz, and Alfonso (2013) have provided reference material helpful for operationalizing the broad and narrow factors assessed by multidimensional intelligence tests, including the UNIT, Raven's Progressive Matrices, Leiter International Performance Scale–Revised (Leiter-R), Matrix Analogies Test (MAT), Beta-III, Comprehensive C-TONI, General Ability Measure for Adults (GAMA), Naglieri Nonverbal Ability Test (NNAT), and the TONI-3. Several of these tests are outdated. While the reference may be helpful for the clinician interested in selecting measures for cross-battery assessment, we stress that it is the clinician's responsibility to understand which subtests measure the same or have similar constructs, how tests are to be administered, and how the results will be interpreted.

In CHC theory, *crystalized intelligence* is narrowly operationalized by language development (LD), lexical knowledge (VL), listening ability (LS), general information (KO), information about culture (K2), general science information (K1), communication ability (CM), oral production and fluency (OP), grammatical sensitivity (MY), foreign language proficiency (KL), and foreign language aptitude (LA). *Fluid Intelligence* is represented by novel prob-lem-solving abilities including general sequential reasoning (RG), induction (I), RQ, Piagetian reasoning (RP), and speed of reasoning (RE). The selection of narrow Gf and Gc abilities to be included in the assessment is to be guided by the examinee's language abil-ity, including degree of hearing loss, cultural factors, and language impairment.

3. *Determine whether broad cognitive domains may be underrepresented by narrow abilities within the core test battery.* Broad abilities are to be represented using at least two narrow subtests that are qualitatively distinct. For example, fluid reasoning may be represented by subtests measuring induction and sequential reasoning. Subtests that are too similar may fail to provide "adequate coverage" of the broader cogni-tive ability (McGrew and Flanaga 1998).

4. *Identify supplemental subtests to be administered in order to assess broad cognitive abilities that are un- or underrepresented in the core battery.* Several nonverbal test batteries listed in step two earlier provide adequate coverage of visual processing, fluid reasoning, processing speed, and long-term memory retrieval abilities. In individual cases where assessment barriers (including hearing impairment, linguistic, cultural, or disruptive behavior) prevent the examinee from partici-pating in a subtest from the core battery, the clinician is challenged to identify alternative subtests (e.g., TONI-III) to supplement or replace the "missing information." In appropriate cases, the PPVT-IV (Dunn and Dunn 2007) may be useful for assessing receptive lan-guage functions in nondeaf individuals.

5. *Administer the core battery and supplemental subtests.* Standard admin-istration procedures are to be used in all cases "unless there are extenu-ating circumstances, and documentation of breaking standardization would be necessary in those circumstances" (Wilhoit and McCallum 2003, 69). Before any accommodations are provided, clinicians should familiarize themselves with any procedures that have empir-ical support, as provided by the test publisher or other researcher.

6. *Complete cross-battery worksheets to derive averaged scores representing each broad cognitive ability.* Wilhoit and McCallum provide work-sheets for calculating averaged scores for broad abilities assessed

by several nonverbal intelligence tests in Appendix B (Wilhoit and McCallum 2003, 74–77). The broad abilities include visual processing, fluid reasoning, long-term retrieval, processing speed, crystalized intelligence, and short-term memory as assessed by the UNIT, Raven's Progressive Matrices, Leiter-R, MAT, Beta III, CTONI, GAMA, NNAT, and TONI-III. Several of these tests have been revised since 2003. Raven's Progressive Matrices may be outdated. Each of the aforementioned tests is built upon the CHC theory and standardized with a mean of 100 and a standard deviation of 15. Furthermore, the calculation suggested by Wilhoit and McCallum is simply an averaging of the narrow abilities used to represent the broad cognitive factor. It is conceivable that this method could be applied to other tests using a common scale, with similar psychometrics and conceptual basis. Extreme caution is warranted in this approach given the error introduced by cross-battery score calculation.

7. *Interpret the results with caution and consideration of their ecological validity and predictive utility.* As we have discussed previously, the clinician's ability to interpret the data with reliability and validity of scores averaged from across multiple instruments is significantly limited and should therefore be avoided where possible. The clinician's level of confidence in the cross-battery validation techniques described here will be highest when, (a) instruments are standardized using appropriate reference groups; (b) instruments are derived using a common theory and structure (e.g., CHC theory of general intelligence); (c) broad cognitive abilities are properly represented by complimentary narrow ability measures; (d) administration procedures described by the test developers are adhered to or are modified to only a minimal degree when necessary and appropriate (and documented); and (e) when the scores obtained from the narrow abilities used to represent the broader factor are statistically similar to one another. In cases in which the narrow ability scores are measured using a common metric and are significantly different from one another (greater than a one standard deviation difference), Wilhoit and McCallum (2003) recommend that each narrow ability is assessed using an additional measure, with the average of the four

narrow subtests used to construe the broad factor. The authors additionally recommend that the scores for each (averaged) broad factor be averaged together; differences between each individual broad factors and the overall average are to be used to interpret the individual's cognitive strengths and weaknesses. The ultimate purpose for assessing cognitive strengths and weaknesses is to provide the examinee or caregivers or both with the information necessary to predict functioning in the real world, and the likelihood to which various accommodations may be helpful for compensating for intellectual or sensory impairment.

Modern Nonverbal Intelligence Measures

It is up to the clinician to decide which measures are appropriate, taking into consideration the purpose, date, and characteristics of the test, and examinee characteristics. Raven's Progressive Matrices is commonly used when the examiner wishes to measure nonverbal intelligence using subtests that do not require motor skills, such as manipulation of blocks or other materials (Braden 1994). Language skills are particularly important for many of these tests and may prohibit their utility (unless instructions can be reliably communicated nonverbally) among individuals with very poor language skills, as is common among many intellectually disabled persons. For this reason, Johnson et al. (2011) suggest integrating observation techniques within the evaluation as measures such as the Wechsler Preschool and Primary Scales of Intelligence or Stanford–Binet Intelligence Scales are highly language dependent and difficult to use with intellectually disabled populations.

Assessments for the Blind

Legal classification for "blindness" varies from state to state, and the term can be used to describe individuals with total blindness, or a level of vision up to the ability to see a target 20 feet away that normally sighted individuals would see 200 feet away. For the purpose of assessment, children with visual impairments can be grouped into three categories (Bauman 1974). The first category includes individuals for whom vision provides no benefit during the test. The second group includes those who have sufficient vision to move or locate large items or to follow an examiner's hand gestures, but who cannot read when the print is enlarged. They may or may not be able to work with form boards. In the third group, the individual shows the ability to read printed words if the type is enlarged, the page is held close to the eyes, or a magnifying lens is used. Sattler (2008) stresses that the clinician must take time to identify what the individual *can* see if residual acuity remains in the person. It may be appropriate to take the hand of a child to lead him or her around the room and accustom him or her to the layout. If glasses, optical prisms, or other lenses are used, the individual must use them during testing. Ensure that the colors of your table and the ground are not the same so that the individual with visual impairment can discriminate between the figure and the ground. Behavioral signs indicating that a child may have (possibly undiagnosed) visual impairment include: rubbing eyes excessively; squinting or covering one eye, difficulty reading or discerning print or objects that are close or far away; losing place while reading; blinking abnormally; crossed eyes; and the presence of red, swollen, inflamed, watery, or encrusted eyes. The individual might complain of difficulty seeing, irritation of the eyes, or report dizziness headaches, nausea, or fatigue following visual tasks.

Studies of the distribution of intelligence scores between children with and without visual impairments have indicated no significant differences between groups on measures of verbal intelligence (Beck and Lindsey 1986). In parallel to the research on children with hearing impairments, these results suggest that it is not necessary to use tests standardized with visually impaired groups when testing children with visual impairments. The Perkins–Binet Tests of Intelligence for the Blind (Davis 1980) were specifically designed to test intelligence in functionally blind children aged 4 to 18 years, although it has been criticized for problems in administration and scoring.

Assessment of intelligence in children with blindness is typically conducted using verbal or haptic or both measures of intelligence. Verbal index scores from verbal and nonverbal measures (e.g., WISC, WAIS, or Woodcock–Johnson Cognitive series) may be used to estimate intelligence. Among children from normative samples, verbal subtests are typically more strongly associated with full-scale intelligence than other indexes. Dekker (1993) devised a haptic variant of the Block Design subtest from the WISC (Third Edition) in which the examinee is given blocks with faces that are smooth, ribbed, or half smooth and half ribbed to measure spatial reasoning skills in the blind. This test composed a part of the Intelligence Test for Visually Impaired Children (ITVIC).

Visual subtests can be administered if the person shows a capacity for learning through visual modality. The results should not be reported as scores figured into the calculation of overall intelligence; rather, they are intended to provide qualitative information only. The interdisciplinary team must agree that the visual items would yield information valuable for the referral question. Several intelligence tests have been devised for use with the blind (e.g., Perkins–Binet), and Braille format versions of other tests (e.g., Woodcock–Johnson Cognitive battery) are available for purchase.

Modern Verbal Intelligence Measures

Landa-Vialard (2015), writing for the American Foundation for the Blind, recommended the WISC-IV, Detroit Test of Learning Aptitude—Fourth Edition, Basic Reading Scale: Braille Edition or Large Type, and the Slosson Intelligence Test–Revised as appropriate for use with blind individuals.

Assessments for Individuals with Motor Impairments

The cognitive assessment of children with motor impairments may be hindered by a variety of potential problems, including poor gait, reduced strength or coordination in one or both hands, orthopedic restraint, ataxia, or self-stimulating behavior. In individuals who can communicate and understand language, there may be impairment in the clarity or rate of speech. When language impairment and motor problems co-occur, as is more likely among intellectually disabled populations, cross-battery approaches to assessment are the only viable approach to intellectual assessment. As with sensory impairments, the clinician is not to penalize the individual's intelligence for his or her motor handicap, though it may be difficult to disentangle the two. In particular, individuals with

cerebral palsy may show heterogeneous deficits in speech, visual and auditory acuity, and motor coordination. Regardless of the etiology of the
motor impairment, a general principle for assessment is that timed tests
requiring some manual dexterity may not be appropriate. If the individual shows additional sensory impairment, tests should be selected based
on the least impaired modality (Sattler 2008).

A variety of testing accommodations are commonly used when working with individuals with motor impairments (Hill-Briggs et al. 2007;
Vig and Sande 2007). Speeded tests may be avoided altogether. Items that
are typically completed by one's self may be administered, and responded
to, orally. When motor functions are partially impaired, use of adaptive
equipment such as pencil grips, handles or clips for documents, or hand
weights for wrists may be sufficient to compensate for the motor impairment. Use of the unaffected nondominant hand may be available in some
cases. In cases in which pain or fatigue are the primary complaints, the
clinician may wish to provide frequent rest breaks, shorter testing sessions
occurring at times when pain is least intense, and ergonomic considerations (e.g., foot rests, seat cushions). Adjustable tables, wide doorways,
and unobstructed room environments are helpful to accommodate
wheelchair sizes.

Completely motor-free tests of intelligence are not available, and
therefore clinicians are encouraged to select verbal and nonverbal tests,
dependent on the individual's aptitude for language, hearing, and vision,
where appropriate. Subtest measures that do not require the use of manipulation or may allow for the use of eye-gaze or verbal responses, and may
be more appropriate for certain types of individuals with motor impairments. It is the clinician's responsibility to establish rapport and devise
a reliable method of communication with the examinee, where possible. If the individual has sensory and motor impairments (more likely
among individuals with severe or profound intellectual disability), many
standardized intelligence tests may be unable to capture the individual's
strengths and weaknesses. For this reason, assessment of adaptive functioning may yield data that are more relevant to the individuals' clinical
prognosis and recommendations.

Summary

Individuals with an intellectual disability and sensory or motor impairments may be difficult to assess for intelligence. The examiner must carefully consider the examinee's sensory-motor limitations and select tests that avoid penalization of their estimated intelligence. The selection of subtests requires experience and an appropriate consideration of how conceptually similar subtests will be combined (preferably with data supporting the concurrent validity of different measures) to represent broader cognitive domains with respect to the individual's functioning in ecologically valid situations. The employment of test accommodations and interpretation of test results are also critical issues in the assessment. These issues require further empirical research and sound clinical judgment in the assessment setting.

CHAPTER 4

Intellectual Disability Recommendations for School and Work Settings

Academic Accommodations for Students with Intellectual Disability

The academic success of students with varying levels of intellectual disability is dependent on individualized accommodations created for different classes and classroom environments. In many instances, children with intellectual disability will need accommodations for particular assignments, subjects, or modes of instruction. Many programs in the past have attempted to devise academic accommodations based on the level of impairment (e.g., mild, moderate, and severe), until recently when these levels of classification were eliminated from the educational programming system (Wehmeyer and Lee 2007). Instead, four intensities were created to base educational need and support for individuals with varying severity of intellectual disability. Intermittent intensity is based on a low or high intensity, as-needed basis throughout schooling and life transitions. Limited intensity is used when individuals require time-limited or short-term support of some staff members and is lower in intensity. The extensive intensity entails regular involvement in some everyday environments (e.g., school, work, home, etc.) and is more long term in nature. Finally, pervasive intensity is utilized when high-intensity, long-term support is needed across many or all environments in an individual's life (Wehmeyer and Lee 2007). Because of this classification system, all academic and occupational accommodations mentioned can apply to individuals with varying severities of intellectual disability based on their needed intensity and duration of support.

General Accommodations

There are many different types of conditions that are accompanied by intellectual disability that may require different types of accommodations depending on the nature of difficulties the child is presenting with. However, there are several different general accommodations that can be made in classroom settings in order to increase information retention and understanding in individuals with intellectual disability. One major accommodation is the teaching material that matches up with real-life experiences that these individuals have underwent. This makes it easier for children with intellectual disability to relate the new information to something that they already have known or experienced, making it more likely for them to retain the information (Shine and Vaccario 2004). This should also be done for skills that have been previously learned in class; new information should be linked to previously learned information in order to ease the learning process. While linking new information to learned information, it is important to keep in mind that a new skill should not be taught until the current skill has been mastered in order to reduce frustration and motivation loss within these students (Shine and Vaccario 2004).

New tasks should be broken into smaller chunks so as to aid the child in learning each step correctly while not overwhelming the child with several steps at once. In doing so, the frustration levels will be reduced and allow for the mastery and understanding of the smaller components that comprise a larger task that would have otherwise been more difficult to learn all at once (Shine and Vaccario 2004). When learning new academic skills or adaptive skills, teachers should provide students with modeling to base their learning from and ample opportunities to practice these skills in real life. This is especially true for adaptive skills. Adaptive skills such as buttoning a shirt or zipping a zipper should be modeled to a student with intellectual disability followed by an opportunity to practice this skill on his or her own. These types of adaptive skills should also be more emphasized with students who need higher intensity and more frequent support in their lives (Shine and Vaccario 2004).

The curriculum for students with intellectual disability should parallel that of normally developing students, but should be presented in a well-organized and easy-to-follow manner in order to reduce confusion and frustration (Gazith 1997). It should progress at the pace of the student so as to optimize the amount of learning and understanding that can be obtained from the material. If a student with intellectual disability is presented with disorganized or less structured content, he or she will become easily confused and may detract that child's ability to learn due to lack of motivation, confusion, and frustration in the situation (Gazith 1997).

Self-determination has been found to be helpful with increasing motivation and overall achievement both within the classroom and in workplaces in children with intellectual disability (Carter et al. 2013). It also aids in the ability for individuals with intellectual disability to determine their own decisions in life and to be able to make those decisions happen. Teachers can help facilitate the development and maintenance of self-determination by providing encouragement and high levels of reinforcement for good work and behavior, and to focus on what the child is doing correctly rather than what the child is doing incorrectly (Timmons et al. 2011). Providing encouragement and positive reinforcement increases not only self-determination but also self-confidence. High self-confidence in individuals with intellectual disability is highly important in their ability to work and gain new information regarding various facets of life (Timmons et al. 2011).

Technology

The use of self-instruction has been found to be useful in teaching individuals with intellectual disability academic and adaptive skills. This mode of teaching has demonstrated significant skill acquisition within the specific population of individuals with intellectual disability (Ayres, Mechling, and Sansosti 2013). This is of particular importance in that once self-instruction has been mastered, an individual with intellectual disability is able to learn a plethora of different skill sets without the need for another individual to model the skill for them (Smith et al. 2015). Technology is pivotal in the acquisition of the skill of self-instruction. In using technology such as an iPad in order to teach themselves different skills, individuals with intellectual disability can learn various skills at the touch of a button. After learning how to navigate these types of technology, they are able to generalize that knowledge in order to learn different skills that are available on that particular mode of technology (Smith et al. 2015).

This mode of teaching has been shown to be particularly useful in learning adaptive skills such as how to brush teeth, button shirts, manage money, and copious other skills (Ayres, Mechling, and Sansosti 2013). There are two types of technology that can be used with individuals: instructional technology and assistive technology. Instructional technology is used in order to aid in the learning and understanding of a new skill or task, such as teaching the skill of keyboarding. Assistive technology is usually used in the ongoing support of learned tasks, such as a vibrating alarm that serves as a reminder for an individual with intellectual disability to take his or her medication.

The one caveat to the use of technology is the need for proper training of the trainers and the trainees. If the trainers or trainees are improperly trained on how to best use the technology, individuals with intellectual disability will be unable to learn as they should via technology, rendering its use as impractical (Ayres, Mechling, and Sansosti 2013). If technology is available to be used in work or school settings, it should be made sure that there is proper training in order to optimize the benefits of using technology with this particular population.

Presentation Mode

Children with intellectual disability learn information in different ways than normally developing students and may require different modes of teaching in order to optimize the learning potential. They have more difficulty in retaining information that was presented to them in a verbal manner (Lifshitz et al. 2011). Teaching children with intellectual disability specific encoding and retrieval strategies may help in the retention of learned verbal information. Strategies such as mnemonics or creating rhymes with information have specifically been shown to help students with intellectual disability create useful associations and therefore aid in retention and understanding. Repetition is also a useful strategy to use with these children. Although this strategy is useful with all types of students, repetition has been shown to aid in the retention of information with students with intellectual disability in particular (Wehmeyer and Lee 2007).

The use of visuals has also been highly helpful in learning for individuals with intellectual disability because they have better visual memory as compared with verbal memory (Lifshitz et al. 2011). Students are able to pair verbal learning with visual representations of the information, allowing them to better understand information and be able to put it into a context that they can physically see, aiding in retention (Wehmeyer and Lee 2007). Visual information also allows these individuals to create visual images and be able to concurrently encode words, places, or objects more deeply. Overhead projectors, pictures, and PowerPoint presentations may aid in the use of visuals for children with intellectual disability (Lifshitz et al. 2011).

The use of role-playing is highly helpful for these individuals in learning skills as it allows them to practice in real life and be able to link their newly learned skills to actual activities that take place (Wehmeyer and Lee 2007). The more times information can be linked to real-life situations, the better the retention and understanding will be.

Social and Coping Skills

Individuals with intellectual disability learn much from their environment via the means of modeling. As such, it is highly beneficial for these students to be able to interact with typically developing peers (Shine and Vaccario 2004). Interaction with these individuals will help children with intellectual disability develop appropriate social and coping skills that can be generalized across several different settings. By interacting with normally developing peers, children with intellectual disability not only learn how to appropriately act within the classroom and with other peers, but also learn coping strategies that are appropriate for reducing frustration in the classroom rather than outwardly expressing frustration in the form of tantrums (Gazith 1997).

Acquisition of proper social skills should not solely be left to peer interaction. Teachers also have a responsibility to directly teach students with intellectual disability social skills that generalize to other situations by directly modeling the behaviors to the students (Shine and Vaccario 2004). The use of concrete behavior plans in order to aid students in deciphering appropriate versus inappropriate behaviors can also be helpful, but may be better instituted with individuals who do not need high frequency or longer-term support. In these cases, it is important for the teachers again to allow the students to have the opportunity to learn these adaptive social skills on their own; if a student is not given an opportunity to practice and learn these skills on his or her own, he or she may become dependent on an adult to give steadfast rules all the time, essentially decreasing the autonomy and independence of a student with intellectual disability (Gazith 1997).

Mathematics

In mathematics, there are certain strategies that may help children with intellectual disability learn basic number skills in an easier fashion in a classroom setting. For these children, teaching them the general rules of number understanding and counting has been shown to be more effective as compared with teaching purely rote learning (Bashash, Outhred, and Bochner 2003). Techniques such as the use of pointing when learning how to count on a number line may help children with intellectual disability learn these skills more readily. Teaching children with intellectual disabilities to check their answers on counting and number-understanding tasks has also been shown to increase learning and the rate of correct mathematical responses (Bashash, Outhred, and Bochner 2003).

Occupational

Teachers usually provide some of the first exposures to work that often set an individual with intellectual disability in a certain career-oriented direction (Timmons et al. 2011). Therefore, it is important for teachers to encourage these individuals not to limit themselves to a certain employment realm. A number of times, early occupational experiences learned via teachers set children in an occupational direction; however, they tend to stick within a narrow realm of work opportunities due to this early refinement and narrowing of occupational learning in school.

Encouraging children to broaden their occupational learning during school may help them gain more knowledge and understanding of the various job opportunities that may be available to them after they finish their education. By providing information on several job opportunities for these children along with encouragement to check all the employment opportunities available to them, they may be able to widen their career choices after college and be able to apply for more jobs that they know to be available to them (Timmons et al. 2011).

Providing students the opportunity to participate in volunteer work around the community may also aid in the students' abilities to determine what types of work they like and what types they do not care for (Shine and Vaccario 2004). It would also give them the opportunity to practice adaptive and academic skills that they have learned in a classroom setting in real-life situations, greatly increasing their ability to utilize these skills in real-world settings.

Accommodations in Vocational Settings

There are a plethora of different accommodations that can be made in vocational settings that are similar to the accommodations that can be made in academic settings, such as the use of technology to learn job skills and training. Learning employment skills and tasks through technology will help increase proficiency in the tasks at hand, thus increasing productivity in the workplace (Ayres, Mechling, and Sansosti 2013). There are other accommodations that are specific to occupational settings that can be employed in order to make the transition to the workforce easier and smoother for individuals with intellectual disability.

Work preparation courses have been shown to be very helpful for individuals with intellectual disability; however, some of these individuals felt pressured when learning these skill sets in the company of customers or other employees and therefore were not as successful in retaining the information needed to utilize the skill effectively in the workplace (Timmons et al. 2011). In order to increase the amount of information retained, learning skills such as how to use a cash register or computer can be taught and learned in sheltered environments within the workplace away from other individuals. This would help the individuals obtain the skills without the unneeded pressure of others as well as making the transition into the workforce easier and less stressful (Timmons et al. 2011). In utilizing these various accommodations as needed on an individual basis, individuals with varying levels of intellectual disability can show personal successes and improvements in many environments that they find themselves in throughout their lives.

CHAPTER 5

Case Studies

Borderline Intellectual Functioning

Zachary is a 12-year-old, right-handed, Caucasian male brought in by his parents for an evaluation due to problems with reading, reading comprehension, and math at home and at school.

History of the Presenting Problem

According to Zachary's mother, Zachary said his first word by age two years and spoke in sentences by age three years. Zachary's mother reports that since he first began speaking, Zachary has had a stutter that occurs sporadically when asking a question. Records indicated he received speech therapy when he was age two to three years, due to delays in speaking. At age five years, Zachary began kindergarten where his mother reported that his kindergarten teacher recommended an occupational therapy evaluation due to concerns over his fine motor skill development. Zachary's mother explained that he attended a secular school where students learn the Hebrew alphabet in kindergarten and the English alphabet in first grade. During first grade, Zachary earned As and Bs in secular and Judaic classes. His teachers commented that he would benefit from reading books over the summer to improve reading speed and comprehension, and that he showed some difficulty understanding math problem-solving concepts when first learned. Zachary's mother further reported that he had difficulty blending English sounds while learning the English alphabet that year in school.

In second grade, Zachary earned Cs and Ds in shoroshim, a Judaic class of Hebrew root words. Zachary also earned two Cs in vocabulary. Records indicated that his teacher recommended that he review math skills over the summer and he strengthen his composition skills. In third grade, he received Cs in reading comprehension, oral reading fluency, vocabulary, spelling, math computation, and math problem solving during his first and second trimesters. It is noted in his report card that he made minimal progress to meet the grade-level standards in writer's workshop. Zachary's teacher recommended reading over the summer to improve reading speed and comprehension. In his Judaic classes, Zachary received two Ds in Torah comprehension, a D and F in shoroshim, and a C in general Judaic knowledge. Zachary's Judaic teacher recommended a review of shoroshim over the summer to be on class level. At the end of the third grade, Zachary took the Iowa Test of Basic Skills and received scores that fell in the 34th percentile in Reading, 23rd percentile in Language, 30th percentile in Mathematics, and 27th percentile in Total. His test profile reported his overall achievement as below average for third grade.

In fourth grade, Zachary earned Cs in reading comprehension, language arts, and math problem solving. Records indicated that Zachary's teacher recommended tutoring for reading comprehension and social studies, noting that his difficulties with reading comprehension were affecting his performance in other classes. In his Judaic classes, Zachary received Cs in Jewish Law and Torah translation skills and reading, and Cs and an F in his Jewish prayer recitation class. Records indicated that he was not on class level in reading, and nightly reading was recommended to improve fluency.

Zachary's mother reported in response to teacher recommendations for tutoring that Zachary began receiving tutoring in the summer between fourth and fifth grades. She reported that he met with a secular tutor once a week for one hour to work on reading, reading comprehension, and math. In addition, he met with a Judaic studies tutor in a group setting four days a week for 45 minutes. In fifth grade, he earned Cs in reading comprehension and math problem solving. He also received a C, a D, and an F in language arts. Records indicated that his teacher recommended reading to improve comprehension and a summer review to gain fundamentals needed for sixth grade. In his Judaic studies, Zachary earned Cs, Ds, and Fs in comprehension, translation, and general knowledge, respectively.

Zachary is currently in the sixth grade. Zachary's mother reported that his secular tutor moved out of the area, so he is now enrolled in an afterschool homework help program, where he stays afterschool for one hour every day and receives assistance with his daily homework. She further explained that his academic difficulties have worsened over time. She reported concerns over his ability to learn new material in school.

Mental Status Exam

Zachary arrived on time for his appointments with his mother. He was dressed casually and was well groomed. Zachary appeared his stated age and was observed to be of average height and weight. He was oriented to person, time, place, and situation with no evidence of formal thought disturbance. He denied experiencing hallucinations and did not make statements consistent with a delusional disorder. Rapport was easily established and maintained; Zachary responded appropriately to questions posed by the clinician. Zachary appeared comfortable conversing with the clinician. His attention and concentration were variable when being spoken to. Zachary's affect appeared to be appropriate to the situation and topic of discussion; he described his mood as being bored. He made appropriate eye contact when spoken to and was cooperative during questioning. There was no evidence of psychomotor slowing. There was evidence of psychomotor agitation, including Zachary exhibiting difficulties with remaining seated. He denied any current suicidal or homicidal ideation, plan, or intent. Zachary recounted an incident of sexual abuse in 2011. Zachary and his father stated that the incident had been reported to the police and this clinician reported the incident to the abuse hotline.

Behavioral Observations

During testing, Zachary was generally cooperative. He would often show evidence of frustration with increasing task difficulty and therefore needed verbal encouragement from the clinician to continue working and to put forth his best effort. A discussion was had with Zachary and his mother after his first session of testing to establish the importance of Zachary putting forth his best effort during testing to produce valid results that would be helpful in understanding Zachary and provide guidance to best respond to his academic difficulties. In addition, Zachary was often visibly agitated in his seat, untying and tying his shoes during testing, and moving in his seat. He often answered items impulsively, switching his answer and requiring prompting to wait and respond appropriately after considering all options and giving each item thought. Zachary also exhibited reluctance to wear his eyeglasses, taking them off often and requiring direction to wear them during testing. Zachary attempted all tasks presented to him. He often appeared to benefit from redirection, praise, and positive reinforcement for his responses. Zachary had no difficulties with transitions from task to task and between breaks and tasks. For more difficult tasks, he would often resist making an attempt or would offer a vague response requiring clarification. On items he perceived as beyond his mastery level, he was reluctant to make a guess unless prompted by the clinician.

Test Results

Wechsler Intelligence Scale for Children—Fifth Edition

The Wechsler Intelligence Scale for Children—Fifth Edition (WISC-V) is a measure of general intellectual functioning. Complete scores are listed as follows:

Verbal Comprehension Subtests	Score	Visual Spatial Subtests	Score
Similarities	6	Block Design	8
Vocabulary	5	Visual Puzzles	10
Working Memory Subtests	**Score**	**Processing Speed Subtests**	**Score**
Digit Span	11	Digit Symbol Coding	7
Picture Span	13	Symbol Search	9
Fluid Reasoning Memory Subtests	**Score**		
Matrix	7		
Figure Weights	8		
Index Scores	**Score**		
Full Scale IQ	81		
Verbal Comprehension	76		

Visual Spatial	94		
Fluid Reasoning	85		
Working Memory	112		
Processing Speed	89		

Expressive Vocabulary Test—Second Edition

The Expressive Vocabulary Test—Second Edition is a measure of expressive vocabulary and word retrieval for Standard American English.

Standard Score	70
Age Equivalent	6:8
Grade Equivalent	1.1

Peabody Picture Vocabulary Test—Fourth Edition

The Peabody Picture Vocabulary Test—Fourth Edition is a measure of receptive vocabulary for Standard American English.

Standard Score	77
Age Equivalent	8:5
Grade Equivalent	2.9

Wide Range Assessment of Memory and Learning—Second Edition

The Wide Range Assessment of Memory and Learning—Second Edition is used to assess memory function.

Core Subtests	Scaled Score	Recognition Subtests	Scaled Score
Story Memory	12	Story Recognition	10
Design Memory	8	Design Recognition	8
Verbal Learning	11	Verbal Learning Recognition	11
Picture Memory	8	Picture Memory Recognition	10
Finger Windows	8		
Number-Letter	12		

(*Continued*)

(Continued)

Delay Recall Subtests	Scaled Score		
Story Memory Recall	12		
Verbal Learning Recall	10		
Index Scores	**Standard Score**		
General Memory	98		
Verbal Memory	108		
Visual Memory	88		
Attention/ Concentration	100		
Verbal Recognition	102		
Visual Recognition	93		
General Recognition	98		
Screening	98		

Woodcock–Johnson Tests of Achievement—Third Edition

The Woodcock–Johnson Tests of Achievement—Third Edition is an extensive test of Zachary's academic achievement in a variety of areas, including tests involving word identification, fluency, and comprehension as well as mathematical calculations and fluency, and spelling and writing fluency.

Clusters	Standard Score	Subtest	Standard Score
Total Achievement	89	Letter-Word Identification	95
Oral Language	94	Reading Fluency	98
Broad Math	95	Story Recall	102
Broad Written Language	85	Understanding Directions	91
Basic Reading Skills	88	Calculation	97
Reading Comprehension	89	Math Fluency	105
Basic Writing Skills	84	Spelling	83
Academic Fluency	96	Writing Fluency	91
Academic Applications	84	Passage Comprehension	76

Academic Knowledge	91	Applied Problems	93
Phon/Graph Knowledge	92	Writing Samples	89
		Story Recall–Delayed	114

Key Math 3

The Key Math 3 is a measure of essential mathematical concepts and skills.

Area	Standard Score	Subtest	Scaled Score
Basic Concepts	82	Numeration	6
Operations	92	Algebra	6
Applications	82	Geometry	8
Total Test	84	Measurement	6
		Data Analysis and Prob.	7
		Mental Comp. and Est.	9
		Add and Subtract	6
		Multiply and Divide	10
		Foundations of Problem Solving	7
		Applied Problem Solving	6

Conners' Continuous Performance Test II

The Conners' Continuous Performance Test II (CPT II) is a computer-based test of visual attention.

Measure	T-Score	Measure	T-Score
Omission Percentage	42	Perseveration Percentage	46
Commissions Percentage	43	Hit Response Time Block Change	43
Hit Reaction Time	46	Hit Standard Error Block Change	51
Hit Reaction Time Standard Error	38	Hit Response Time ISI Change	44
Variability	38	Hit Standard Error ISI Change	41
Detectability	49	ADHD Score	34
Response Style	41	Neurological Score	-

Wisconsin Card Sorting Test

The Wisconsin Card Sorting Test (WCST) is used to assess executive functioning, the ability to shift and maintain problem-solving strategies for abstract problems when given feedback. A computerized 128-card version of the test was used for this evaluation.

Measure	Raw Score	T-Score
Total Categories Completed	6	
No. Trials to Complete 1st Category	11	
Total Number Correct	70	
Total Percent Correct	75	
Total Number Errors	23	55
Total Percent Errors	25	52
Total of Perseverative Responses	10	57
Total of Perseverative Errors	10	56
Total Percent Perseverative Errors	11	54
Total Non-Perseverative Error	13	51
Total of Other Responses	0	
Percent Conceptual Level Response	66	50
Total of Failure to Maintain Sets	0	
Learning to Learn Score	−3.52	

Finger Tapping Test

Finger Tapping is a test of motor speed and hand coordination. Zachary's performance was within normal limits. Complete scores are as follows:

Hand	Time
Dominant	41
Non-Dominant	36

Trail Making Tests A and B

The Trail Making tests measure cognitive flexibility, sequencing ability, and visual-motor speed. Trail A is a measure of visual scanning and motor speed. The examinee is asked to draw connecting lines between numbered circles in sequential order (1 to 2, 2 to 3, etc.). Trail B is similar to Trail A but also measures the ability to shift between different kinds of sequencing tasks. The examinee is asked to alternate between numbers and letters, in order, while connecting the circles (1 to A, 2 to B, 3 to C, etc.).

Test	Time	Errors
Trails A	26	0
Trails B	94	2

Conners 3 Parent Rating Scales

Parent Form

The Conners 3 Parent Rating Scale provides information about a child's behavior from a parent's point of view.

Zachary's mother's test scores appear as follows:

Scale	T-Score	
Inattention	69	
Hyperactivity/Impulsivity	79	
Learning Problems	87	
Executive Functioning	53	
Aggression	64	
Peer Relations	48	
Global Index Total	76	
DSM-IV Inattentive	58	
DSM-IV Hyperactivity/Impulsivity	77	
DSM-IV Conduct Disorder	67	
DSM-IV Oppositional Defiant Disorder	61	
Validity Scales	**Raw Score**	**Cut-Off Score**
Positive Impression	0	≥4
Negative Impression	0	≥3
Inconsistency Index	4	≥6
Symptom Counts		
Inattentive ADHD Symptoms	2	≥6
Hyperactive/Impulsive ADHD Symptoms	6	≥6

(*Continued*)

(Continued)

Conduct Disorder Symptoms	3	≥3
Oppositional Defiant Disorder Symptoms	2	≥4
Functional Impairment		
Schoolwork or Grades	3	3 = Sig. Impairment
Friendships/Relationships	0	3 = Sig. Impairment
Home Life	2	3 = Sig. Impairment
Conners' ADHD Probability Percentage	71%	

Parent Form

The Conners 3 Parent Rating Scale provides information about a child's behavior from a parent's point of view. Zachary's father completed the form and responded in a consistent fashion.

Zachary's father's test scores appear as follows:

Scale	T-Score	
Inattention	72	
Hyperactivity/Impulsivity	72	
Learning Problems	78	
Executive Functioning	54	
Aggression	52	
Peer Relations	48	
Global Index Total	76	
DSM-IV Inattentive	62	
DSM-IV Hyperactivity/Impulsivity	69	
DSM-IV Conduct Disorder	50	
DSM-IV Oppositional Defiant Disorder	58	
Validity Scales	**Raw Score**	**Cut-Off Score**
Positive Impression	1	≥4
Negative Impression	0	≥3
Inconsistency Index	5	≥6
Symptom Counts		
Inattentive ADHD Symptoms	3	≥6
Hyperactive/Impulsive ADHD Symptoms	4	≥6
Conduct Disorder Symptoms	0	≥3
Oppositional Defiant Disorder Symptoms	1	≥4

Functional Impairment		
Schoolwork or Grades	2	3 = Sig. Impairment
Friendships/Relationships	0	3 = Sig. Impairment
Home Life	1	3 = Sig. Impairment
Conners' ADHD Probability Percentage	56%	

Teacher Form

The Conners' 3 Teacher Rating Scale provides information about a child's behavior from a teacher's point of view.

Zachary's Hebrew studies teacher's test scores are as follows:

Scale	T-Score	
Inattention	73	
Hyperactivity/Impulsivity	69	
Learning Problems	74	
Executive Functioning	68	
Aggression	50	
Peer Relations	53	
Global Index Total	75	
DSM-IV Inattentive	66	
DSM-IV Hyperactivity/Impulsivity	71	
DSM-IV Conduct Disorder	46	
DSM-IV Oppositional Defiant Disorder	65	
Validity Scales	**Raw Score**	**Cut-Off Score**
Positive Impression	1	≥4
Negative Impression	1	≥3
Inconsistency Index	10	≥6
Symptom Counts		
Inattentive ADHD Symptoms	4	≥6
Hyperactive/Impulsive ADHD Symptoms	7	≥6
Conduct Disorder Symptoms	0	≥3
Oppositional Defiant Disorder Symptoms	2	≥4
Functional Impairment		
Schoolwork or Grades	3	3 = Sig. Impairment
Friendships/Relationships	0	3 = Sig. Impairment
Conners' ADHD Probability Percentage	93%	

Zachary's Secular studies teacher's test scores are as follows:

Scale	T-Score	
Inattention	60	
Hyperactivity/Impulsivity	56	
Learning Problems	68	
Executive Functioning	64	
Aggression	50	
Peer Relations	43	
Global Index Total	59	
DSM-IV Inattentive	56	
DSM-IV Hyperactivity/Impulsivity	58	
DSM-IV Conduct Disorder	46	
DSM-IV Oppositional Defiant Disorder	55	
Validity Scales	**Raw Score**	**Cut-Off Score**
Positive Impression	2	≥4
Negative Impression	1	≥3
Inconsistency Index	3	≥6
Symptom Counts		
Inattentive ADHD Symptoms	1	≥6
Hyperactive/Impulsive ADHD Symptoms	4	≥6
Conduct Disorder Symptoms	0	≥3
Oppositional Defiant Disorder Symptoms	1	≥4
Functional Impairment		
Schoolwork or Grades	2	3 = Sig. Impairment
Friendships/Relationships	0	3 = Sig. Impairment
Conners' ADHD Probability Percentage	39%	

Personality Inventory for Youth

The Personality Inventory for Youth (PIY) is an objective measure used for child personality assessment.

Scale	T-Score	Scale	T-Score
VAL (Validity)	81	RLT (Reality Distortion)	37
INC (Inconsistency)	44	Rlt1 (Feelings of Alienation)	37

FB (Dissimulation)	60	Rlt2 (Hallucination/ Delusion)	41
DEF (Defensiveness)	53	SOM (Somatic Concern)	36
COG (Cognitive Impairment)	57	Som1 (Psychosomatic)	38
Cog1 (Poor Achieve./Memory)	42	Som2 (Muscle Tension/ Anxiety)	40
Cog2 (Inadequate Abilities)	61	Som3 (Preoccupation with Disease)	38
Cog3 (Learning Problems)	75	DIS (Psychological Discomfort)	42
ADH (Impulsivity/Distractible)	56	Dis1 (Fear/Worry)	36
Adh1 (Brashness)	49	Dis2 (Depression)	57
Adh2 (Distractible/ Overactive)	56	Dis3 (Sleep Disturbance)	38
Adh3 (Impulsivity)	57	WDL (Social Withdrawal)	47
DLQ (Delinquency)	47	Wdl1 (Social Introversion)	46
Dlq1 (Antisocial)	50	Wdl2 (Isolation)	51
Dlq2 (Dyscontrol)	47	SSK (Social Skill Deficits)	48
Dlq3 (Noncompliance)	43	Ssk1 (Limited Peer Status)	53
FAM (Family Dysfunction)	46	Ssk2 (Conflict with Peers)	41
Fam1 (Parent-Child Conflicts)	56		
Fam2 (Parent Maladjustment)	41		
Fam3 (Marital Discord)	43		

Personality Inventory for Children—Second Edition

The Personality Inventory for Children—Second Edition (PIC-2) is an objective measure used for child personality assessment.

Zachary's mother's test scores appear as follows:

Scale	T-Score	Scale	T-Score
INC (Inconsistency)	44	RLT (Reality Distortion)	59
FB (Dissimulation)	52	Rlt1 (Developmental Deviate)	55
DEF (Defensiveness)	52	Rlt2 (Hallucination/ Delusion)	62
COG (Cognitive Impairment)	73	SOM (Somatic Concern)	45
Cog1 (Inadequate Abilities)	68	Som1 (Psychosomatic)	48

(Continued)

(Continued)

Cog2 (Poor Achievement)	70	Som2 (Muscle Tension/ Anxiety)	42
Cog3 (Developmental Delay)	67	DIS (Psychological Discomfort)	50
ADH (Impulsivity/ Distractible)	49	Dis1 (Fear/Worry)	60
Adh1 (Disruptive Behavior)	49	Dis2 (Depression)	46
Adh2 (Fearlessness)	48	Dis3 (Sleep/Death Concern)	45
DLQ (Delinquency)	45	WDL (Social Withdrawal)	<40
Dlq1 (Antisocial)	46	Wdl1 (Social Introversion)	40
Dlq2 (Dyscontrol)	43	Wdl2 (Isolation)	42
Dlq3 (Noncompliance)	48	SSK (Social Skill Deficits)	54
FAM (Family Dysfunction)	44	Ssk1 (Limited Peer Status)	54
Fam1 (Member Conflicts)	46	Ssk2 (Conflict with Peers)	52
Fam2 (Parent Maladjustment)	43		

Zachary's father's test scores appear as follows:

Scale	T-Score	Scale	T-Score
INC (Inconsistency)	41	RLT (Reality Distortion)	50
FB (Dissimulation)	43	Rlt1 (Developmental Deviate)	55
DEF (Defensiveness)	54	Rlt2 (Hallucination/ Delusion)	44
COG (Cognitive Impairment)	64	SOM (Somatic Concern)	48
Cog1 (Inadequate Abilities)	68	Som1 (Psychosomatic)	43
Cog2 (Poor Achievement)	59	Som2 (Muscle Tension/ Anxiety)	57
Cog3 (Developmental Delay)	55	DIS (Psychological Discomfort)	46
ADH (Impulsivity/ Distractible)	49	Dis1 (Fear/Worry)	43
Adh1 (Disruptive Behavior)	51	Dis2 (Depression)	49
Adh2 (Fearlessness)	<40	Dis3 (Sleep/Death Concern)	45
DLQ (Delinquency)	45	WDL (Social Withdrawal)	<40
Dlq1 (Antisocial)	46	Wdl1 (Social Introversion)	40
Dlq2 (Dyscontrol)	43	Wdl2 (Isolation)	42
Dlq3 (Noncompliance)	48	SSK (Social Skill Deficits)	52

FAM (Family Dysfunction)	41	Ssk1 (Limited Peer Status)	57
Fam1 (Member Conflicts)	42	Ssk2 (Conflict with Peers)	43
Fam2 (Parent Maladjustment)	43		

Test of Memory Malingering

The Test of Memory Malingering (TOMM) is used to assess the degree of effort displayed by a client on memory tasks.

Trial	Score
Trial 1	46
Trial 2	50
Retention Trial	50

Discussion

Results of the neuropsychological evaluation suggest that Zachary put forth adequate effort throughout the evaluation. Zachary's overall intellectual functioning was found to be in the Below Average range, with his nonverbal abilities being stronger than his verbal abilities. His overall level of achievement was found to be in the Low Average range, consistent with his measured intelligence, and his cognitive functioning was found to be in the Average range, above his measured intelligence. His overall memory functioning was found to be in the Average range. Zachary's ability to complete a novel task while receiving feedback was found to be in the Average range.

Results from objective personality tests indicated that he responded in an open and honest fashion. Zachary endorsed areas indicating that he has difficulties with learning, including being held back in school, having difficulty with reading, and having speech problems in the past.

Results from the questionnaires given to Zachary's parent's indicate that he has difficulty with cognitive impairment and experiences poor achievement, endorsing trouble with being able to get him to do his school lessons, reading being a problem for him, not completing his homework on time, not enjoying reading, not doing well in arithmetic classes, being hard for him to make good grades, not enjoying working with numbers, getting extra help due to problems in learning, and school being difficult for him. They also indicated that Zachary has difficulties with hyperactive and impulsive behaviors and learning problems, endorsing items describing Zachary exhibiting behaviors including blurting out answers before the question has been completed, constantly moving, getting overstimulated, having difficulty waiting his turn, and squirming or fidgeting in seat. She also endorsed Zachary not understanding what he reads, having trouble with reading, needing extra explanation of instructions, and reading slowly with a lot of effort.

Zachary's teachers suggested that he is dealing with difficulties in learning and exhibiting symptoms of inattention along with hyperactive and impulsive behaviors.

Based on records provided and test results, a diagnosis of Borderline Intellectual Functioning was considered. This category is used when the focus of clinical attention is associated with borderline intellectual functioning, that is an intelligence quotient (IQ) in the 71 to 84 range. These IQ scores describe uncommonly low intellectual ability, which are not low enough to qualify for a diagnosis of mental retardation. This classification describes a group comprising about seven percent of the general population that falls into an area of delayed intellectual, emotional, or adaptive functioning that is on the edge of mental retardation but does not actually qualify for that specific diagnosis. Like mental retardation, borderline intellectual functioning is a classification, not a specific disease. Deficits often go unnoticed until children reach school settings or other demanding and unfamiliar environments. There, the condition manifests itself in poor academic performance, lack of attention to tasks, and behavioral problems, which may stem from frustration and emotional immaturity.

Zachary and his parents reported that he has been struggling in school. He has performed below average on standardized testing and has been receiving poor grades in his classes. He requires additional help to complete his homework and struggles with his coursework.

On the WISC-V, Zachary obtained a Full Scale IQ (FSIQ) of 81, which is associated with borderline intellectual functioning. He has displayed long-standing academic difficulties, obtaining many Cs, Ds, and Fs in elementary school. Achievement test results exhibit abilities within the Low Average range. Thus, he meets criteria for Borderline Intellectual Functioning.

Intellectual Disability, Mild

John is a five-year-old, right-handed male referred for a neuropsychological evaluation to document his intellectual capacity due to reported cognitive, academic, and behavioral difficulties following a diagnosis of bacterial meningitis when he was 2.5 months old.

History of the Presenting Problem

John's mother reported that he started exhibiting symptoms of fever, irritability, and breathing and feeding difficulties when he was 73 days old. John's mother indicated that he was transferred to the hospital via ambulance and was admitted to the pediatric intensive care unit. The medical records indicate that he looked "dusky," was not breathing well, and had tachycardia with a heart rate of 220. Approximately 2.5 days after admission, test results were positive for Group B Streptococcus Meningitis. He was prescribed 1- to 28-day-course of antibiotics and results of a magnetic resonance imaging (MRI) revealed multifocal nonhemmorhagic lacunar infarction in the bilateral basal ganglia. A CAT scan was performed, revealing periventricular hypodensities in the periventricular white matter adjacent to the anterior horns of the lateral ventricle. The medical records indicated that John had additional medical diagnoses of septicemia, low birth weight, swelling limbs, esophageal reflux, hypertension, and adverse effects of corticosteroids. It was suggested that he be sent to a developmental clinic for developmental follow-up.

John's mother reported significant concerns regarding his cognitive, academic, and behavioral functioning. She reported: delayed speech and language, learning difficulties, memory problems, hyperactivity, a short attention span, difficulty expressing himself, following instructions, and sitting still. She indicated that John's Headstart teacher noticed that he was performing below his peers.

John was referred by his Headstart teacher for an evaluation on to determine his eligibility for Exceptional Student Services. His expressive and receptive language abilities fell in the Impaired range and he evidenced deficits in cognitive processing. Results of the Developmental Assessment of Young Children, Second Edition (DAYC-2), suggested a general developmental quotient in the Below Average range (Standard Score (SS) = 82). His social-emotional and physical development, both gross and fine, were in the Average range. He consequently received an Individual Education Plan for the 2015 to 2016 school year.

Mental Status Exam

John arrived on time for the appointment with his mother. He was dressed casually and was well groomed. He appeared his stated age and was observed to be of average height and weight. He was oriented to person, time, place, and situation with no evidence of formal thought disturbance. Rapport was easily established and maintained; John had difficulty understanding the questions posed by the clinician. He appeared comfortable conversing with the clinician and demonstrated a desire to be open and honest. His attention and concentration were inconsistent throughout the interview, as he was easily distracted and had difficulty sitting still until the clinician offered him play doh to occupy him while answering the interview questions. When discussing school and friends, he became excited stating that he enjoyed his friends and playing outside. When asked what he would like to change about himself, he said nothing. He made appropriate eye contact when spoken to and was cooperative during the interview. There was no evidence of psychomotor slowing or agitation. He denied any history or current abuse as well as suicidal or homicidal ideation, plan, or intent.

Behavioral Observations

During the initial testing session, John had difficulty separating from his mother in order to begin testing. He was slow to warm up to the clinician; however, after a few minutes, he appeared calm and comfortable. John was generally cooperative and willing to attempt all tasks presented to him during all testing sessions. He often evidenced frustration with tasks of increasing difficulty, as he would cover his face with his hands or hit himself in the head. He would evidence difficulty holding conversation with the clinician, as questions posed by the clinician were answered with sentences that did not reflect an answer to the question. John needed constant redirection and verbal encouragement from the clinician to answer and put forth effort. He did benefit from praise, positive reinforcement, and redirection to the tasks presented. During one session, he continually asked when the testing was going to be completed and redirected his attention to tying his shoes to avoid completing the task. In addition, John had difficulty remaining seated throughout the testing session, exhibiting fidgety behaviors. He enjoyed receiving stickers and benefited from receiving praise from the clinician following each session.

School Observations

A school observation revealed that John had difficulty initiating tasks posed by the homeroom teacher. It would take him much longer to start his assignments, as he was out of his chair to get a drink of water or wash his hands at the sink located in the classroom. John did not appear actively engaged during the lectures. John's homeroom teacher separately assisted him following a classroom activity, discussing a worksheet the class had completed earlier. John was easily distracted from tasks despite being willing to participate in group activities. When the teacher asked the students to share what they had done over the weekend, he answered with an illogical response that was difficult to comprehend. John was able to follow one- to two-step directions posed by the teacher; however, when multiple directions were asked, John appeared to having difficulty following directions. When split into small groups, John had to constantly be redirected to begin a reading program on a laptop. During lunch, John interacted and was friendly with his peers. He moved up and down from his seat throughout lunch while laughing and interacting with his peers. John appears to have many friends and is well liked by his classmates. He appeared happy and kind to the children around him.

Test Results

Wechsler Preschool and Primary Scale of Intelligence—Fourth Edition

The Wechsler Preschool and Primary Scale of Intelligence—Fourth Edition (WPPSI-IV) is a measure of general intellectual functioning.

Verbal Comprehension Subtests	Score	Perceptual Reasoning Subtests	Score
Information	3	Block Design	5
Similarities	6	Object Assembly	3
Fluid Reasoning	**Score**	**Working Memory**	**Score**
Matrix Reasoning	7	Picture Memory	3
Picture Concept	7	Zoo Locations	8
Processing Speed	**Score**		
Bug Search	8		
Cancellation	5		
Verbal Comprehension	73		
Visual Spatial	67		
Fluid Reasoning	85		
Working Memory	75		
Processing Speed	79		
Full Scale	72		

Wide Range Assessment of Memory and Learning—Second Edition

The Wide Range Assessment of Memory and Learning—Second Edition is used to assess memory function.

Core Subtests	Scaled Score	Recognition Subtests	Scaled Score
Story Memory	10	Story Recognition	9
Design Memory	7	Design Recognition	6
Verbal Learning	7	Verbal Learning Recognition	7
Picture Memory	11	Picture Memory Recognition	6
Finger Windows	7		
Number-Letter	12		

Delay Recall Subtests	Scaled Score		
Story Memory Recall	9		
Verbal Learning Recall	6		
Index Scores	**Standard Score**		
General Memory	91		
Verbal Memory	91		
Visual Memory	94		
Attention/Concentration	97		
Verbal Recognition	85		
Visual Recognition	78		
General Recognition	78		
Screening	91		

Woodcock–Johnson Test of Cognitive Abilities—Fourth Edition

The Woodcock–Johnson IV Test of Cognitive Abilities (WJ-IV COG) is a test that assesses many aspects of cognitive functioning, including visual spatial thinking, auditory processing, fluid reasoning, and processing speed.

Clusters	Standard Score	Subtest	Standard Score
General Intellectual Ability (gia)	79	Oral Vocabulary	80
Gf-Gc Composite	72	Number Series	76
Comp-Knowledge (Gc)	81	Verbal Attention	93
Fluid Reasoning	73	Letter-Pattern Matching	79
Short-Term Work Mem	77	Phonological Processing	85
Cognitive Efficiency	74	Story Recall	89
		Visualization	85
		General Information	87
		Concept Formation	82
		Numbers Reversed	72

Woodcock–Johnson Tests of Achievement—Fourth Edition

The Woodcock–Johnson Tests of Achievement—Fourth Edition (WJ-IV ACH) is an extensive test of John's academic achievement in a variety of areas, including tests involving word identification, fluency and comprehension as well as mathematical calculations and fluency, and spelling and writing fluency.

Clusters	Standard Score	Subtest	Standard Score
Reading	86	Letter-Word Identification	85
Broad Reading	82	Applied Problems	70
Basic Reading Skills	82	Spelling	92
Reading Fluency	80	Passage Comprehension	90
Mathematics	68	Calculation	80
Broad Mathematics	69	Writing Samples	80
Math Calculation Skills	75	Word Attack	79
Written Language	83	Oral Reading	78
Broad Written Language	78	Sentence Reading Fluency	78
Written Expression	76	Math Facts Fluency	76
Academic Skills	82	Sentence Writing Fluency	79
Academic Applications	80		
Brief Achievement	82		
Broad Achievement	79		

Expressive Vocabulary Test—Second Edition

The Expressive Vocabulary Test—Second Edition is a measure of expressive vocabulary and word retrieval.

Standard Score	80
Age Equivalent	4:1
Grade Equivalent	<K.0

Peabody Picture Vocabulary Test—Fourth Edition

The Peabody Picture Vocabulary Test—Fourth Edition is a measure of receptive vocabulary.

Standard Score	84
Age Equivalent	4:3
Grade Equivalent	<K.0

Beery-Buktenica Developmental Test of Visual-Motor Integration, Sixth Edition

The Beery Visual-Motor Integration (VMI) is designed to assess the extent to which individuals can integrate their visual and motor abilities (eye–hand coordination). There are two subtests administered: the Visual Perception subtest, which requires John to identify picture outlines and parts of a picture, as well as pointing to matching shapes. There are only minimal motor requirements on this subtest.

	Beery VMI	Visual Perception	Motor Coordination
Raw Scores	13	15	12
Standard Scores	90	90	81
Scaled Scores	8	9	6
Percentiles	25	30	10

Conners' 3 Parent Rating Scales

Parent Form

The Conners' 3 Parent Rating Scale provides information about a child's behavior from a parent's point of view.

Scale	T-Score
Inattention	89
Hyperactivity/Impulsivity	69
Learning Problems	71
Executive Functioning	62
Aggression	61
Peer Relations	44
Global Index Total	65
DSM-IV Inattentive	87
DSM-IV Hyperactivity/Impulsivity	70

(Continued)

(Continued)

DSM-IV Conduct Disorder	52	
DSM-IV Oppositional Defiant Disorder	60	
Validity Scales	**Raw Score**	**Cut-Off Score**
Positive Impression	1	≥4
Negative Impression	0	≥3
Inconsistency Index	11	≥6
Symptom Counts		
Inattentive ADHD Symptoms	21	≥6
Hyperactive/Impulsive ADHD Symptoms	17	≥6
Conduct Disorder Symptoms	1	≥3
Oppositional Defiant Disorder Symptoms	6	≥4
Functional Impairment		
Schoolwork or Grades	3	3 = Sig. Impairment
Friendships/Relationships	0	3 = Sig. Impairment
Home Life	0	3 = Sig. Impairment
Conners' ADHD Probability Percentage	98%	

Teacher Form

The Conners' 3 Teacher Rating Scale provides information about a child's behavior from a teacher's point of view. John's homeroom teacher completed the form.

John's homeroom teacher's test scores are as follows:

Scale	T-Score
Inattention	75
Hyperactivity/Impulsivity	48
Learning Problems	78
Executive Functioning	66
Aggression	48
Peer Relations	43
Global Index Total	56
DSM-IV Inattentive	63
DSM-IV Hyperactivity/Impulsivity	46
DSM-IV Conduct Disorder	44
DSM-IV Oppositional Defiant Disorder	50

Validity Scales	Raw Score	Cut-Off Score
Positive Impression	1	≥4
Negative Impression	1	≥3
Inconsistency Index	5	≥6
Symptom Counts		
Inattentive ADHD Symptoms	6	≥6
Hyperactive/Impulsive ADHD Symptoms	2	≥6
Conduct Disorder Symptoms	0	≥3
Oppositional Defiant Disorder Symptoms	1	≥4
Functional Impairment		
Schoolwork or Grades	3	3 = Sig. Impairment
Friendships/Relationships	0	3 = Sig. Impairment
Conners' ADHD Probability Percentage	81%	

Personality Inventory for Children—Second Edition

The PIC-2 is an objective measure used for child personality assessment.

Scale	T-Score	Scale	T-Score
INC (Inconsistency)	55	RLT (Reality Distortion)	56
FB (Dissimulation)	49	Rlt1 (Developmental Deviate)	50
DEF (Defensiveness)	40	Rlt2 (Hallucination/Delusion)	60
COG (Cognitive Impairment)	71	SOM (Somatic Concern)	45
Cog1 (Inadequate Abilities)	72	Som1 (Psychosomatic)	48
Cog2 (Poor Achievement)	63	Som2 (Muscle Tension/Anxiety)	42
Cog3 (Developmental Delay)	67	DIS (Psychological Discomfort)	50
ADH (Impulsivity/Distractible)	65	Dis1 (Fear/Worry)	54
Adh1 (Disruptive Behavior)	68	Dis2 (Depression)	46
Adh2 (Fearlessness)	48	Dis3 (Sleep/Death Concern)	54
DLQ (Delinquency)	53	WDL (Social Withdrawal)	46
Dlq1 (Antisocial)	46	Wdl1 (Social Introversion)	45

(Continued)

(Continued)

Dlq2 (Dyscontrol)	43	Wdl2 (Isolation)	50
Dlq3 (Noncompliance)	61	SSK (Social Skill Deficits)	52
FAM (Family Dysfunction)	46	Ssk1 (Limited Peer Status)	57
Fam1 (Member Conflicts)	46	Ssk2 (Conflict with Peers)	43
Fam2 (Parent Maladjustment)	49		

Adaptive Behavior Assessment Scale—Second Edition

Parent Forms

The Adaptive Behavior Assessment Scale (ABAS-II) measures skills that are important to everyday life. It comprehensively, validly, and reliably describes the degree to which individuals display normal adaptive behavior, and skills.

The mother's scores are as follows:

Skill Areas	Scaled Score	Skill Area	Scaled Score
Communication	7	Leisure	8
Community Use	6	Self-Care	6
Functional Academics	7	Self-Direction	6
Home Living	6	Social	8
Health and Safety	5		
Composite	**Composite Score**		
GIA	65		
Conceptual	76		
Social	87		
Practical	71		

Discussion

Current neuropsychological testing revealed overall intellectual abilities within the Borderline range of functioning. John's visual information processing and abstract reasoning skills were a relative strength for him as was his categorical reasoning ability. He displayed difficulties with visual spatial information and did not have a good general factual knowledge base. On a second measure of cognitive functioning, including visual spatial thinking, auditory processing, fluid reasoning, and processing speed, John performed in the Borderline range. He performed well when recall details of a story and on measure of verbal attention. He had some difficulty when asked to repeat numbers in reverse order.

On an assessment of memory, John exhibited an ability to maintain focus and recall information that was presented to him both in an auditory and visual manner. He was able to recall details of a story and recognize the details after a delay. He did not perform as well when asked to recall a list of words. He showed some difficulty with drawing previously presented designs, both before and after a delay but did better when presented with a picture and asked what differed from a previously presented picture. John appears to perform better with contextual clues.

On achievement measures, John performed in the Borderline to Low Average range of functioning. He displayed the most difficulty on measures of math, both timed and untimed. When asked to quickly read sentences or write simple sentences he performed in the Borderline range. John's performance was in the Average range when asked to complete simple sentences and spell words. John's expressive and receptive language abilities fell within the Borderline range of functioning. Measures of visual motor abilities, visual perception, and motor coordination all fell within the Below Average range of functioning.

Behaviorally, John's mother indicated clinically significant concerns in the areas of inattention and learning problems. Specifically, she indicated that he had trouble staying focused, had a short attention span, avoided or disliked things that took a lot of effort and were not fun, had trouble concentrating, did not pay attention to details, was easily distracted, gave up easily on difficult tasks, and had trouble keeping his mind on work or play for long. She endorsed items indicating that John had poor reading, poor arithmetic, and forgot things already learned. On a second measure, his mother indicated that John was Below Average in reading, writing, spelling, and learning the processes of mathematics. She indicated receptive and expressive language limitations, inadequate common sense, and problematic academic achievement that is recognized and being addressed in the classroom. In addition, she indicated that John had poor memory.

His teacher endorsed items indicating difficulties with inattentive symptoms, symptoms of having a short attention span, being sidetracked easily, giving up easily on difficult tasks, getting bored, having trouble concentrating, difficulty with changing from one task to another, and having trouble keeping his mind on work or play for long. His home-room teacher also endorsed learning problems, including reading, spelling, and arithmetic. In addition, the teacher indicated that he does not remember or understand what he reads, as well as forgets things he has previously learned.

On a measure assessing John's skills that are important to everyday life, his mother's endorsements indicated that the client's overall level of adaptive functioning was in the Borderline range of functioning. The mother's endorsements reflected that the client's overall level of adaptive functioning was in the Below Average range. She noted difficulties in that he was unable to write his own first and last name, and was unable to state time and day of favorite television shows. She expressed concern that he was unable to listen closely for at least five minutes when people talk, was unable to repeat stories or jokes after hearing them from others, and was unable to end conversations appropriately.

Overall, given the test results, John falls within the intellectual disabilities, mild category. Academically, he performs above expected levels given his intellectual abilities, but he shows difficulty with expressive and receptive language as well as adaptive living skills.

Intellectual Disability, Mild

Joel is a 44-year-old, right-handed Jamaican male referred by his mother for a comprehensive neuropsychological evaluation to determine his level of cognitive functioning.

History of the Presenting Problem

The background information regarding Joel's presenting problem was compiled from an interview with Joel and his mother. His mother functions as power of attorney for general matters, including homestead property. She answered questions that Joel was not able to answer.

Joel's mother reported that he grew up in Jamaica, and indicated that he has had a long-standing difficulty with learning and communication since he was very young. She described the initial communication deficits as differentiating between similar-sounding words. For example, she would tell him to bring her an item, and he would bring a similar-sounding object. She reported that he had difficulties hearing throughout his childhood due to persistent ear infections, which eventually created a hole in his eardrum that had to be surgically repaired when he was at age 13 years. She indicated that, as a baby and young child, he did not seek out social interaction with his parents or peers. Furthermore, when he went to school, his mother stated that many of his teachers expressed concerns regarding his level of learning in that they observed a desire to learn, but he would often become frustrated because of a low processing speed and difficulties in understanding or learning the material. She indicated that his teachers recommended a different style of teaching, and that he receive a formal evaluation to assess his cognitive functioning. Joel's mother then reported that she sought an evaluation through the Micro College Care Centre in Jamaica. She described this process of attaining an evaluation as being very difficult due to the general deficits in resources for mental health issues in Jamaica at that time, particularly for families from a lower socioeconomic standing. Results of the evaluation indicated deficits in reading, mathematics, verbal comprehension, perceptual organization, and receptive and expressive language. According to the report, his speech articulation and hearing were within normal limits. He was administered the WSIC (Revised). He received an index score of 60 on Conceptualization and Reasoning Ability, a 51 on the Visual Spatial Index, a 54 on the Sequencing and Concentration Index, and a 51 on the Acquired Knowledge Index.

Joel's mother stated that he never received formal interventions, services, or accommodations to remediate these deficits. She indicated that she utilized informal assistance from other teachers in the community for private tutoring sessions. However, she stated that this did little to ameliorate his deficits, as these teachers were unsure of the proper way to instruct him. She reported that he attended formal schooling until fourth grade in Jamaica. She indicated that he received grades of Ds and that the teachers passed him because they were unsure with how to best serve his needs. He then attended a preparatory school, which was founded by a teacher whom she knew and trusted. She indicated that he attended classes there until seventh grade, but that this was primarily just to give him a daily activity. He then reportedly accompanied his father, who was a mechanic and his reported primary caretaker, to work and assist with the vehicle repairs. When his father passed away in 2012, Joel's mother reported that she became concerned about Joel's future and per the recommendations of his primary care physician, sought a neurology consult, where an MRI scan was conducted. Results of the MRI revealed no significant findings.

Joel is seeking a comprehensive evaluation to clarify diagnoses and to evaluate his current cognitive and adaptive levels of functioning to make functional recommendations.

Mental Status Exam

Joel and his mother arrived on time for the majority of his appointments. He was dressed appropriately and his appearance was neat for all appointments. He appeared his stated age and was of average height and weight for his age. He maintained minimal eye contact. He was oriented to person, but had limited orientation to time, place, and situation. He appeared to have minimal insight into why he was being evaluated. He displayed no evidence of formal thought disturbance. He denied any current hallucinations and did not make statements consistent with a delusional disorder. His affect appeared to be congruent with his mood, which was reported as "okay." Rapport was slightly slow in being established, as he appeared guarded when interacting with the examiner. However, as the interview progressed, he seemed to become more comfortable in interacting with the examiner. He occasionally needed prompting from the examiner or his mother to answer questions or for them to be rephrased. This is not thought to be due to a lack of compliance but rather a diminished level of comprehension. However, he answered the questions in an open fashion. His tone and articulation were diminished and his prosody displayed an inconsistent pattern, in which sometimes he would speak fast, and other times would require prompting from the individual. There was no evidence of psychomotor agitation or retardation. He did not display difficulties sitting still for long periods of time. He displayed appropriate behavior throughout the interview. He reported that he felt stressed and worried when his father died, particularly regarding who would take care of him. He affirmed feeling sad or irritable primarily surrounding the time when his father passed away and reported that these feelings have improved. He denied a history or current of physical, verbal, or sexual abuse, which was confirmed by his mother. He also denied past or current suicidal or homicidal ideation, plan, or intent, which was also confirmed by his mother.

Behavioral Observations

Joel was cooperative throughout testing, and required minimal breaks. He maintained a pleasant demeanor throughout testing. He evidenced a high frustration tolerance as items on each task got progressively more difficult. On tasks that were more difficult, he would often hum to himself before giving an answer. He demonstrated a deficit in his ability to understand directions, and would often indicate that he understood but then was unable or had difficulty completing the task according to the directions. The examiner often had to repeat or rephrase the instructions several times. He would guess on items he did not understand, choosing to give an answer over making sure he had the correct answer. He also exhibited a deficit in responding to feedback both from the examiner and from computerized tests. He demonstrated that he understood that he had the incorrect answer by shaking his head. However, he struggled with adjusting the way he completed the task, even if the feedback indicated that he was incorrect. In tasks of abstract problem solving, he was unable to verbalize the strategy that he was using to complete the task, preferring to complete the task even if his answers were predominantly incorrect.

Test Results

Wechsler Adult Intelligence Scale—Fourth Edition

The Wechsler Adult Intelligence Scale—Fourth Edition (WAIS-IV) is a measure of general intellectual functioning.

Verbal Comprehension Index	Score	Perceptual Reasoning Index	Score
Similarities	1	Block Design	4
Vocabulary	3	Matrix Reasoning	3
Information	2	Visual Puzzles	5
Working Memory Index	**Score**	**Processing Speed Index**	**Score**
Digit Span	1	Symbol Search	2
Arithmetic	2	Coding	2
Index Scores	**Score**		
Full Scale IQ	50		
Verbal Comprehension	52		
Perceptual Reasoning	65		
Working Memory	53		
Processing Speed	56		

Woodcock–Johnson Cognitive—Third Edition

The Woodcock–Johnson Cognitive—Third Edition (WJC-III) is a test that assesses many aspects of cognitive functioning including visual spatial thinking, auditory processing, fluid reasoning, and processing speed.

Clusters	Standard Score	Subtest	Standard Score
GIA	49	Verbal Comprehension	60
Verbal Ability	60	Visual-Auditory Learn	53
Thinking Ability	59	Spatial Relations	81
Cognitive Efficiency	53	Sound Blending	66
Phonemic Awareness	70	Concept Formation	60
Working Memory	62	Visual Matching	53
Delayed Recall	1	Numbers Reversed	65
		Incomplete Words	83
		Aud. Work Memory	72
		Vis-Aud Learn Delayed	47

Wechsler Memory Scale—Fourth Edition

The Wechsler Memory Scale—Fourth Edition (WMS-IV) is a test of an individual's visual and verbal memory functioning.

Subtests	Score	Subtests	Score
Logical Memory I	1	Logical Memory II	1
Designs I	7	Designs II	9
Verbal Paired Associates I	3	Verbal Paired Associates II	3
Visual Reproduction I	7	Visual Reproduction II	7
Index Scores	**Score**		
Auditory Memory	49		
Visual Memory	85		
Immediate Memory	63		
Delayed Memory	66		

Woodcock–Johnson Tests of Achievement—Third Edition

The Woodcock–Johnson Tests of Achievement—Third Edition is an extensive test of academic achievement in a variety of areas, including tests involving word identification, fluency and comprehension as well as mathematical calculations and fluency, and spelling and writing fluency.

Clusters	Standard Score	Subtest	Standard Score
Total Achievement	31	Letter-Word Identification	50
Oral Language	48	Reading Fluency	54
Broad Math	24	Story Recall	62
Broad Written Language	36	Understanding Directions	54
Broad Reading	41	Calculation	22
Brief Reading	39	Math Fluency	47
Brief Math	31	Spelling	43
Math Calculation Skills	30	Writing Fluency	58
Brief Writing	35	Passage Comprehension	42
Written Expression	27	Applied Problems	36
Academic Fluency	49	Writing Samples	15
Academic Applications	30	Story Recall–Delayed	52
Academic Skill	41		

Expressive Vocabulary Test

The Expressive Vocabulary Test (EVT) is a test of the expressive (spoken) vocabulary of children and adults. It is used as an achievement test of expressive vocabulary attainment for standard English and as a screening test of verbal ability.

Raw Score	Standard Score
99	48

Peabody Picture Vocabulary Test, Fourth Edition

The Peabody Picture Vocabulary Test, Fourth Edition (PPVT-4) is a test of the receptive (hearing) vocabulary of children and adults.

Raw Score	Standard Score
72	57

Conners' Continuous Performance Test III

The Conners' CPT–III is a computerized visual performance test that assesses attention and impulse control.

Measure	T-Score
Detectability	72
Omissions	62
Commissions	76
Perseverations	53
Hit Reaction Time	44
Hit Reaction Time Standard Deviation	65
Variability	55
Hit Response Time Block Change	65
Hit Reaction Time ISI Change	35
Level of Likelihood of Attention Deficits	High
Response Pattern Indicates Issues Related to:	Inattentiveness (some)
	Impulsivity (strong)
	Sustained Attention (some)
	Vigilance (some)

Conners' Continuous Auditory Test of Attention

Conners' Continuous Auditory Test of Attention (CATA) is a computerized auditory performance test that assesses attention and impulse control. Scores are listed in the following:

Measure	T-Score
Detectability	83
Omissions	46
Commissions	90
Perseverative Commissions	86
Hit Reaction Time	46
Hit Reaction Time Standard Deviation	61
Hit Reaction Time Block Change	37
Level of Likelihood of Attention Deficits	High
Response Pattern Indicates Issues Related to	Inattentiveness (strong)
	Impulsivity (some)
Advantage to Right or Left Ear	No
Issue with Auditory Mobility	No

Wisconsin Card Sorting Test

The WCST is used to assess executive functioning, namely the ability to shift and maintain problem-solving strategies for abstract problems when given feedback. A computerized 128-card version of the test was used for this evaluation.

Measure	Raw	T-Score
Total Categories Completed	0	-
No. of Trials to Complete 1st Category	129	-
Total Number Correct	31	-
Total Percent Correct	24	-
Total Number Errors	97	21
Total Percent Errors	76	22
Total Number Perseverative Responses	59	26
Total Number Perseverative Errors	53	24

(*Continued*)

(Continued)

Total Percent Perseverative Errors	41	22
Total Number Nonperseverative Errors	44	25
Total Number Other Responses	22	-
Percent Conceptual Level Response	6	23
Total of Failure to Maintain Sets	1	-
Learning to Learn Score	N/A	-

Category Test

The Category Test is a computerized evaluative tool used to measure nonverbal concept formation and the ability to shift and maintain problem-solving strategies.

Number of Errors	Heaton SS	T-Score
119	2	26

Trail Making Tests A and B

The Trail Making tests measure cognitive flexibility, sequencing ability, and visual-motor speed. Trails A is a measure of visual scanning and motor speed. The examinee is asked to draw connecting lines between numbered circles in sequential order (1 to 2, 2 to 3, etc.). Trail B is similar to Trail A but also measures the ability to shift between different kinds of sequencing tasks. The examinee is asked to alternate between numbers and letters, in order, while connecting the circles (1 to A, 2 to B, 3 to C, etc.).

Test	Time	Errors	T-Score
Trail A	226	7	22
Trail B	300	N/A	N/A

Tactual Performance Test

The Tactual Performance Test is used to assess sensory and motor function, including recognition of three-dimensional shapes by touch, spatial-motor problem solving, and memory for tactile and spatial information. The client is blindfolded and asked to place blocks of various shapes into corresponding slots in a board as quickly as possible. A 10-figure vertical board was used for this evaluation.

Hand	Seconds Per Block	T-Score
Dominant	300	34
Nondominant	120	38
Both Hands	38	40
Total time	92.94	35
Memory	XXX	33
Location	XXX	41

Finger Tapping Test

Finger Tapping is a test of motor speed and hand coordination.

Hand	Time	T-Score
Dominant	56	58
Nondominant	58.6	72

Test of Memory Malingering

The TOMM is used to assess the degree of effort displayed by a client on memory tasks.

Trial	Score
Trial 1	41
Trial 2	50
Retention Trial	50

Discussion

Results of the current neuropsychological evaluation revealed that Joel put forth adequate effort. His overall intellectual functioning was in the Very Impaired range, and his general memory functioning was in the Impaired range. In terms of academic abilities, his overall level of achievement was in the Very Impaired range. His verbal comprehension and vocabulary ability was in the Impaired range. When allotted additional time, his scores did not significantly improve. His expressive language skills fell in the Very Impaired range; whereas, his receptive language skills fell in the Below Average range. He demonstrated deficits in executive functioning and attention, including difficulty in abstract problem solving, adjusting performance based on feedback, cognitive flexibility, and sequencing. His nonverbal, spatial abilities to put blocks in their correct locations using his hands independently were in the Below Average range. When using both of his hands, his score was in the low end of the Average range. He did not demonstrate motor deficits.

According to the report of Joel's mother, he has always needed supervised care. He was able to perform simple adaptive skills on his own, such as doing his own laundry or making tea; however, this has required significant training and instruction to be able to independently carry out these tasks. For more complicated tasks, he continues to require instruction where the steps are broken down for him in manageable increments. He has a long-standing history of deficits in communication, functional academic skills, social or interpersonal skills, work, and self-direction. He also has a long-standing difficulty of recognizing and adjusting to the social norms and nuances in his interactions, which can cause him frustration. It is difficult to determine how far he was able to independently progress in school due to his mother's report that he was passed through to the next class by his teachers, although he formally stopped attending school following seventh grade.

Joel's intellectual ability (Full Scale Intelligence Quotient (FSIQ) = 50) indicates that he has significantly lower than average intellectual functioning. Per the report of his mother, he received grades of Ds throughout his education, which was used to pass him through to the next grade. Although he received informal tutoring, he was reportedly unable to adequately master the material. His overall academic achievement (WJ-ACH Total Achievement = 31) confirms a global deficit in academic proficiency. In terms of adaptive skills, he is able to perform simple household tasks, and basic hygiene. Therefore, a diagnosis of Mental Retardation, Mild is warranted.

Intellectual Disability, Moderate

Linda is a 21-year-old, right-handed, Caucasian female referred by her mother to assess her cognitive and vocational capabilities.

History of the Presenting Problem

Linda's mother reported that at the age of two years, Linda began to evidence difficulty with balance, gait, and controlled movement. She reported that prior evidence of difficulties was chalked up to the possibility of a developmental delay but at this time, evaluation by a specialist led to a diagnosis of cerebellar atrophy and ataxia. An evaluation from when Linda was seven years old indicated a Stanford Binet Verbal IQ of 70, Receptive score of 69, and Expressive score of 60. Records indicate that Linda has been placed on an IEP since first grade and received Exceptional Student Education Services as Orthopedically Impaired. While grades were not provided because of her special education placement, according to academic transcripts Linda repeated third grade due to failure to pass the courses. Academic transcripts reported that Linda was administratively placed into a higher grade until sixth grade.

An MRI of the brain without contrast at age 11 years indicated that Linda had marked prominence of the cerebellar fissures compared to the cerebellar folia, indicating the presence of volume loss and cerebellar atrophy. There also was involvement of the cerebellar vermis and both hemispheres; however, the brain stem appeared spared and the supratentorial elements appeared within normal limits.

According to medical records, at age 13 years, Linda received an MRI of her cervical, thoracic, and lumbar spine without IV contrast. Reports indicated that cerebellar atrophy was evidenced, along with thoracolumbar scoliosis with the upper thoracic component convex to the right and the lower lumbar component convex to the left. Her doctor also reported that in the upper thoracic spine, the cord was draped along the right side of the spinal canal, and in the mid- and lower thoracic spine, the cord was draped along the left side of the spinal canal due to her severe scoliosis. At the age of 15 years, Linda underwent a spinal fusion in order to correct her severe scoliosis.

Linda attended high school and graduated with a special high school diploma. Academic records indicate that at age 18 years Linda underwent a psychoeducational evaluation. Results indicated that on the Stanford Binet Fifth Edition she obtained an FSIQ of 50, Nonverbal IQ of 56, and a Verbal IQ of 49. On the Woodcock–Johnson Test of Achievement—Third Edition, the clinician indicated that although Linda was in the

12th grade at the time of testing, her academic skills in reading, writing, and math ranged from first to third grade equivalence. Linda evidenced an overall Adaptive Behavior Composite within the intellectually deficient range (56 from parent, 59 from teacher) on the Vineland Adaptive Behavior Scales—Second Edition.

At the time of this evaluation, Linda was attending a special program where she was working on her reading and spelling capabilities. However, she was 21 years old and was going to age out of the program at the end of the academic year. Thus, Linda's mother is seeking an evaluation to determine her current level of functioning and vocational capabilities.

Tests Results

Stanford Binet Intelligence Scales—Fifth Edition

The Stanford Binet Intelligence Scales—Fifth Edition (SB-5) measures a person's general verbal and nonverbal intellectual abilities.

Nonverbal Index	Score	Verbal Index	Score
Fluid Reasoning	1	Fluid Reasoning	3
Knowledge	1	Knowledge	5
Quantitative Reasoning	6	Quantitative Reasoning	4
Visuospatial	4	Visuospatial	2
Working Memory	4	Working Memory	1
Index Scores	**Score**		
Full Scale IQ	54		
Nonverbal IQ	56		
Verbal IQ	56		
Fluid Reasoning	53		
Knowledge	60		
Quantitative Reasoning	72		
Visuospatial	59		
Working Memory	57		

Wechsler Memory Scale–Fourth Edition

The WMS-IV is a test of an individual's visual and verbal memory functioning.

Subtests	Score	Subtests	Score
Logical Memory I	1	Logical Memory II	2
Designs I	5	Designs II	6
Verbal Paired Associates I	6	Verbal Paired Associates II	7
Visual Reproduction I	2	Visual Reproduction II	6
Index Scores	**Score**		
Auditory Memory	64		
Visual Memory	67		
Immediate Memory	56		
Delayed Memory	67		

Woodcock Johnson Tests of Cognitive Abilities—Fourth Edition

The WJ-IV COG is a test that assesses many aspects of cognitive functioning, including visual spatial thinking, auditory processing, fluid reasoning, and processing speed.

Clusters	Standard Score	Subtest	Standard Score
GIA	<40	Oral Vocabulary	<40
Gf-Gc Composite	45	Number Series	54
Comp-Knowledge	<40	Verbal Attention	41
Fluid Reasoning	57	Letter-Pattern Matching	53
S-Term Working Memory	<40	Phonological Processing	47
Cognitive Efficiency	41	Story Recall	53
		Visualization	64
		General Information	<40
		Concept Formulation	70
		Numbers Reversed	45

Woodcock–Johnson Tests of Achievement—Fourth Edition

The Woodcock–Johnson Tests of Achievement—Fourth Edition is an extensive test of Linda's academic achievement in a variety of areas, including tests involving word identification, fluency and comprehension as well as mathematical calculations and fluency, and spelling and writing fluency.

Clusters	Standard Score	Subtest	Standard Score
Reading	<40	Letter-Word Identification	<40
Broad Reading	<40	Applied Problems	41
Basic Reading Skills	<40	Spelling	<40
Reading Fluency	<40	Passage Comprehension	48
Mathematics	42	Calculation	51
Broad Mathematics	<40	Writing Samples	64
Math Calculations Skills	<40	Word Attack	42
Written Language	43	Oral Reading	40
Broad Written Language	<40	Sentence Reading Fluency	<40
Written Expression	48	Math Facts Fluency	<40
Academic Skills	<40	Sentence Writing Fluency	<40
Academic Fluency	<40		
Academic Applications	44		
Brief Achievement	<40		
Broad Achievement	<40		

Wide Range Achievement Test—Fourth Edition

The Wide Range Achievement Test—Fourth Edition (WRAT-4) is a screening measure of academic achievement in the domains of word reading, sentence comprehension, spelling, and arithmetic.

Subtests	Standard Score	Grade Level
Reading	58	2.0
Sentence Comprehension	55	1.2
Spelling	57	1.5
Arithmetic	61	2.9
Reading Comprehension	57	.

Peabody Picture Vocabulary Test, Fourth Edition

The PPVT-4 is a measure of receptive vocabulary.

Raw	Standard Score	Grade Level	Age Level
108	42	K.9	6:7

EVT, Second Edition

The EVT-2 is a measure of expressive vocabulary and word retrieval.

Raw	Standard Score	Grade Level	Age Level
69	49	<K.0	5:7

Conners' Continuous Performance Test II

The Conners' CPT-III is a computerized visual performance test that examines sustained attention and impulse control.

Measure	T-Score
Detectability	54
Omissions	53
Commissions	56
Perseverations	47
Hit Reaction Time	45
Hit Reaction Time Standard Deviation	69
Variability	58
Hit Reaction Time Block Change	56
Hit Reaction Time Interstimulus Interval Change	61

Conners' CATA

Conners' CATA is a computerized auditory performance test that assesses auditory processing and attention.

Measure	T-Score
Detectability	55
Omissions	47

(*Continued*)

(Continued)

Commissions	52
Perseverations	50
Hit Reaction Time	76
Hit Reaction Time Standard Deviation	52
Hit Reaction Time Block Change	50
Level of Attention Deficits	None
Response Pattern	Mild Inattentive
Auditory Laterality Issue with Auditory Mobility	Slight Left None

Wisconsin Card Sorting Test

The WCST is used to assess executive functioning, namely the ability to shift and maintain problem-solving strategies for abstract problems when given feedback.

Measure	Raw	T-Score
Total Categories Completed	2	-
No. of Trials to Complete 1st Category	10	-
Total Number Correct	49	-
Total Percent Correct	38	-
Total Number Errors	79	23
Total Percent Errors	62	25
Total Number Perseverative Responses	49	21
Total Number Perseverative Errors	44	<20
Total Percent Perseverative Errors	34	<20
Total Number Nonperseverative Errors	35	31
Total Number Other Responses	16	-
Percent Conceptual Level Response	23	26
Total of Failure to Maintain Sets	1	-
Learning to Learn Score	−40.0	-

Category Test

The Category Test is a computerized evaluative tool used to measure nonverbal concept formation and the ability to shift and maintain problem-solving strategies.

Number of Errors	Heaton SS	T-Score
106	4	26

Stroop Color-Word Test

The Stroop Color-Word Test is used to measure an individual's concentration and ability to switch between different kinds of cognitive tasks.

Measure	Raw	T-Score
Word	28	16
Color	31	28
Color/Word	9	26
Interference	−5.71	40

Test of Memory Malingering

The TOMM is used to assess the degree of effort displayed by a client on memory tasks.

Trial	Score
Trial 1	34
Trial 2	49
Retention Trial	50

Discussion

Neuropsychological testing revealed intellectual abilities within the Very Low range of functioning. Linda experienced difficulties completing tasks involving expressive language, such as reading words and explaining solutions. Nonverbally, she evidenced difficulties assembling pieces into designs and tapping blocks. Her abilities to solve verbal and nonverbal problems with inductive and deductive reasoning, to see patterns and spatial orientations, and to store and transform short-term memory were in the Very Low range. She also evidenced difficulties with numerical problem solving and pictured relationships and did not have a fund of school-based general knowledge. Her performance on a measure assessing visual spatial thinking, auditory processing, and fluid reasoning fell in the Very Low range of functioning. She exhibited difficulties in efficiently storing information for later retrieval, and hold orally presented information in immediate awareness and utilize it within a few seconds. Her ability to perceive, synthesize, and discriminate auditory stimuli was well below age-expected levels as was her ability to perceive, analyze, and synthesize visual patterns. She exhibited difficulties with reasoning and solving novel problems.

Memory functioning was in some ways a strength for Linda. With regard to memory functioning, Linda performed within the Very Low range of functioning. She exhibited difficulties storing and recalling items presented in both a visual and verbal manner. She was unable to successfully recall details of short stories or recreate visual designs. However, her ability to recall pairs of words and recall placement of design cards was a relative strength for her.

Academically, Linda exhibited extreme difficulties on all measures of reading, writing, and mathematics. When required to complete fluency measures, she was unable to do so quickly as she has motor difficulties and does not have the fundamental knowledge to complete the task. On a second, untimed academic measure she exhibited difficulty with word reading, sentence comprehension, spelling, and arithmetic. She is currently performing between the first and second grade levels in all achievement areas. On measures of receptive and expressive language, Linda performed well below her expected age level.

Scores on sustained attention measures, both visual and auditory, were within normal limits. Measures of executive functioning fell within the Impaired range, as she exhibited difficulties with shifting and maintaining problem-solving strategies and utilizing feedback to solve abstract problems. Her nonverbal concept formation and ability to switch between different types of cognitive tasks also fell within the Impaired range. A test of malingering showed that she was putting forth maximum effort throughout testing.

Intellectual Disability, Moderate

Steven, a four-year-old, Caucasian male, was referred for an evaluation to determine his cognitive and intellectual functioning as his parents expressed concerns about his developmental delays in the areas of language, motor, social, and adaptive functioning. Steven's parents maintained that he exhibited defiant behaviors (e.g., tantrums, noncompliance) at home and in the community.

History of the Presenting Problem

Doctors discovered a congenital heart condition in Steven during the 24th week of pregnancy and he was born eight weeks premature. At the time of delivery, he was transferred to the neonatal intensive care unit (NICU), where he remained for his first two months of life and underwent surgery to repair an open connection between the left pulmonary artery and the aorta (i.e., persistent ductus arteriosus) because her body did not close the connection naturally. Steven was also born with agenesis of the corpus callosum. Steven's corpus callosum, the structure that connects the two hemispheres of the brain, is completely absent, a deficit that may lead to difficulty making connections between functions controlled by both hemispheres (e.g., learning to ride a bicycle, acquisition of speech, and language development).

Regarding major developmental milestones, he first sat at around eight months and walked at 24 months. He began smiling at two months and crawling at one year. Language development is still described as extremely limited, and aside from the use of these titles for mom and dad, Steven communicates by making noises (e.g., whining, using single-syllable sounds), gesturing (e.g., pointing, reaching), and leading adults to things. Steven currently drinks from a "sippy cup," can hold it with two hands, and demonstrates a preference for placing his cup in a particular spot on the table. Steven is not fully potty-trained, and is currently utilizing pull-ups to aid in the process.

A psychological evaluation was conducted to determine eligibility for her current school placement when he was two years, 11 months old. The evaluation revealed that he had progressed with early intervention but continued to display delays in the areas of cognitive, communication, motor, social-emotional, and self-help skills. Steven is currently in prekindergarten and his classroom includes students with varying levels of developmental delays as well as students who are typically developing for their ages. Steven displays poor social interactions with classmates and was described as often playing alone and taking toys from other children with no apparent awareness of the importance of sharing or playing cooperatively. Rather than interacting with the other children, he tends to seek attention and affection from his teachers.

Test Results

Battelle Developmental Inventory, Second Edition

Adaptive (ADP)			Communication (COM)		
Subdomain	Scaled Score	Age Equivalent	Subdomain	Scaled Score	Age Equivalent
Self-Care	1	1:8	Receptive Communication	1	1:8
Personal Responsibility	2	2:0	Expressive Communication	1	0:11

Personal-Social (P-S)			Cognitive (COG)		
Subdomain	Scaled Score	Age Equivalent	Subdomain	Scaled Score	Age Equivalent
Adult Interaction	8	3:7	Attention and Memory	1	0:10
Peer Interaction	1	<2:0	Reasoning and Academic Skills	1	<2:0
Self-Concept and Social Role	1	2:0	Perception and Concepts	1	1:7

Motor (MOT)		
Subdomain	Scaled Score	Age Equivalent
Gross Motor	2	2:1
Fine Motor	1	1:10
Perceptual Motor	2	2:0

Domain Scores			
Domain	Developmental Quotient	Percentile Rank	95% Confidence Interval (CI)
Adaptive (ADP)	58	<1	53–69
Personal-Social (P-S)	74	4	70–80
Communication (COM)	55	<1	51–63
Motor (MOT)	57	<1	52–68
Cognitive (COG)	55	<1	51–65
BDI-2 Total	50	<1	48–54

PPVT-4	
Standard Score	52
95% Confidence Interval	47–61
Percentile	<1
Stanine	1
Age Equivalent	<2 years

Vineland Adaptive Behavior Scales, Second Edition (Vineland II) Teacher Rating Form			
Domains/Subdomains	Composite/ V-Scores	Percentile Rank	Adaptive Level
Adaptive Behavior Composite	52	<1	Low
Communication	54	<1	Low
Receptive	8	–	Low
Expressive	6	–	Low
Written	8	–	Low
Daily Living Skills	63	1	Moderately Low
Personal	7	–	Low
Academic	10	–	Moderately Low
School Community	10	–	Moderately Low
Socialization	60	<1	Moderately Low
Interpersonal Relationships	6	–	Low
Play and Leisure Time	7	–	Low

(*Continued*)

(Continued)

Coping Skills	10	–	Moderately Low
Motor Skills	55	<1	Low
Gross Motor Skills	8	–	Low
Fine Motor Skills	6	–	Low

Vineland Adaptive Behavior Scales, Second Edition (Vineland-II) Parent/Caregiver Rating Form			
Domains/Subdomains	Composite/ V-Scores	Percentile Rank	Adaptive Level
Adaptive Behavior Composite	55	<1	Low
Communication	59	<1	Low
Receptive	11	–	Moderately Low
Expressive	5	–	Low
Written	9	–	Low
Daily Living Skills	53	<1	Low
Personal	6	–	Low
Domestic	10	–	Moderately Low
Community	7	–	Low
Socialization	59	<1	Low
Interpersonal Relationships	7	–	Low
Play and Leisure Time	7	–	Low
Coping Skills	9	–	Low
Motor Skills	59	<1	Low
Gross Motor Skills	9	–	Low
Fine Motor Skills	7	–	Low
Maladaptive Behavior Index	18	–	Elevated
Internalizing Problems	20	–	Elevated
Externalizing Problems	14	–	Average

Discussion

In order to assess Steven's current cognitive and intellectual functioning, he was administered the Battelle Developmental Inventory, Second Edition (BDI-2). The Cognitive domain involves items that look at thinking, reasoning, and early learning skills. Steven achieved a developmental quotient (DQ) in the Well Below Average range on the Cognitive domain as compared to same-age peers. Scores were consistently in the Well Below Average range across the attention and memory (ability to engage in an environmental setting for a length of time and recall short and long-term information), reasoning and academic skills (evaluate critical thinking and basic academic milestones), and perception and concepts (evaluate knowledge of relationships among stimuli and compare and contrast objects) subdomains. Steven's delay in achieving age-appropriate cognitive milestones has a detrimental impact on his early success in school-related activities and academic instruction should be focused on a two-year-old level.

Steven scored within the Well Below Average range overall on the Motor domain of the BDI-2. This area assesses gross motor skills such as walking, jumping, and running, as well as coordinated movements (e.g., throwing, using stairs). Steven displayed gross motor skills equivalent to that of a two-year-old. For example, he is able to walk without support and walk up and down at least four stairs. However, he has difficulty walking on a line, jumping with both feet leaving the ground, and throwing a ball. Fine motor skills focus on the control and coordination of small muscles in the arms and hands that allow performance of increasingly complicated and precise tasks. Steven's score on the fine motor subdomain was also well below average for his age and reflected trouble with skills such as pointing with one finger, grasping a pencil, and stringing beads. He was, however, able to demonstrate skills such as extending a toy to the examiner and removing forms from a form board successfully. On the Beery-Buktenica Developmental Test of Visual-Motor Integration, Sixth Edition, he was only able to hold the end of a crayon with a fist and to scribble lightly with a crayon for two strokes. He exhibited difficulty grasping, orienting to the task, and sustaining attention to instructions, and was unable to complete the reproduction of any of the test designs. Both parent and teacher reports of gross and fine motor skills on the Vineland Adaptive Behavior Scales, Second Edition (Vineland-II) also indicated that he is functioning at a low adaptive level.

The Personal-Social domain of the BDI-2 assesses abilities and characteristics that allow a child to engage in meaningful social interaction with adults and peers and to develop his or her own self-concept and social role. Steven demonstrated a personal strength on the adult inter-action (quality and frequency of a child's interactions with adults) sub-domain; he connects with caregivers, teachers, and other adults in order to get his basic needs and immediate interests met. Steven is able to utilize several nonverbal tactics to interact with adults (e.g., reaching, leading, giving objects, pointing, making sounds) to gain attention or to obtain a tangible benefit (e.g., drink, food, toy). His development of self-awareness, personal knowledge, self-worth, coping skills, and sensitivity to other's needs and feelings was found to be well below average on the Self-Concept and Social Role subdomain. Steven's forming friendships, responding to and initiating social contacts with peers, and cooperating were well below average, as measured by the Peer Interaction subdomain. His father indicated elevated concerns within the area of socialization on the Vineland-II, reporting that he very frequently chooses to play by himself and does not seek the company of other children. His teacher also reported socialization skills below the expected adaptive level.

Steven's communication skills fell well within the Below Average range. Receptively, he exhibited receptive language facility equivalent to children less than two years of age. Similarly, he achieved a score within the well Below Average range on the PPVT-4. When presented with visual stimuli and asked to discriminate among items, Steven often became dis-tracted by extraneous details (e.g., feeling of paper, sound of tapping) or hyper-focused on items of tangential interest (e.g., animals) in lieu of completing the task. Expressive language, which is the use of sounds, words, or gestures to relate information to others, was also well below average on the BDI-2 Expressive Communication subdomain. Both par-ent and teacher ratings of his receptive, expressive, and written communi-cation skills on the Vineland-II indicate that his functioning is well below expectations for his age.

The Adaptive domain involves two areas relating to Steven's daily liv-ing and self-care skills. Her ability to complete age-appropriate self-care milestones (e.g., eating, dressing, toileting, grooming) was found to be within the Well Below Average range. His ability to assume responsibility for his actions (e.g., putting away toys) and move around in the envi-ronment safely and productively (e.g., avoiding a hot stove) were also well below average for his age. He has difficulty with age-appropriate behaviors such as indicating illness and demonstrating caution (e.g., running across a street). Overall, Steven is currently demonstrating adaptive functioning consistent with most two-year-old children. Both parent and teacher reports of adaptive functioning on the Vineland-II further indicate that his levels of daily adaptive living skills at home, school, and in the community are markedly low for his age.

Taken together, Steven's developmental delays across all domains (e.g., motor, communication, personal-social, cognitive, adaptive) reflect a total BDI-2 developmental quotient in the Well Below Average range as compared to his same-age peers. In addition, his Adaptive Behavior Composite on the Vineland-II teacher and parent rating forms point to consistent delays in communication, daily living skills, motor skills, and socialization.

Intellectual Disability, Severe

Daniel is a 23-year-old, Caucasian male referred by his mother to determine if he is eligible to enroll in a new assisted-living facility.

History of the Presenting Problem

Daniel's mother stated that he was born prematurely at 26 weeks' gestation weighing two pounds, two ounces. Records revealed that he was born with significant medical problems. At birth, he received the following medical diagnoses: respiratory distress syndrome, bronchopulmonary dysplasia, apnea of prematurity, hyperbilirubinemia of prematurity, patent ductus arteriosus, encephalomalacia, chemical rickets, and retinopathy of prematurity. According to the mother, he remained in the NICU for the first three months of his life. He received a diagnosis of cerebral palsy, spastic quadriparesis at two years of age. As per his mother's report, early developmental milestones were reached as follows: showed a response to his mother at two months; followed objects with his eyes at eight months, and rolled over "one way only" at seven months. Currently, Daniel presents as a physically limited young adult who has poor control over his head and extremities. Moreover, he requires complete assistance from his caregiver and he is bound to a wheelchair. According to his medical records, Daniel possesses generalized low muscle tone, but when excited, his tone increases and he becomes stiff and tight.

Mental Status Exam

He arrived on time for the appointment accompanied by his mother. He was well groomed, clean, and his appearance was neat. Daniel appeared younger than his reported age. He displayed signs of discomfort during the session by moving his hands, writhing, and vocalizing. According to his mother, he becomes distressed when surrounded by strangers and loud noises. Daniel stopped vocalizing and moving after his mother made physical contact with him and praised his patience. Moreover, Daniel appeared comforted by his mother's presence in the room. In general, the client appears to have impaired mental control functions.

Behavioral Observations

Daniel was wheelchair bound, nonverbal, and completely dependent on his caregivers. According to his mother, Daniel is currently taking antiseizure medications, and his reaction to the medication manifests as increased sleepiness throughout the day. Daniel arrived awake to the testing session but fell asleep approximately 20 minutes into the administration. To establish rapport and obtain a baseline measure of Daniel's functional level, the examiner asked him to follow her finger from left to right, to look at the painting on the wall, and to look at the wall and back to the examiner's face. Additionally, the examiner tried to obtain responses from the client using blinking and vocalizations. He was only able to look at the colorful painting on the wall by following the examiner's index finger. Daniel was not aware of the various stimuli presented to him during the testing session. The examiner attempted to get his attention several times by calling his name and by touching him slightly on his hand. No responses were obtained from the client at any point during the interview.

Test Results

Adaptive Behavior Assessment System—Second Edition

Parent Form

The ABAS measures skills that are important to everyday life. It comprehensively, validly, and reliably describes the degree to which individuals display normal adaptive behavior, and skill.

The mother's scores are as follows:

Skill Areas	Scaled Score	Skill Area	Scaled Score
Communication	1	Leisure	1
Community Use	1	Self-Care	1
Functional Academics	1	Self-Direction	1
Home Living	1	Social	1
Health and Safety	1		
Composite	**Composite Score**		
GAC	41		
Conceptual	49		
Social	55		
Practical	40		

Peabody Picture Vocabulary Test—Fourth Edition

The Peabody Picture Vocabulary Test—Fourth Edition is a measure of receptive vocabulary.

Standard Score	20
Grade Equivalent	<K.0

Wide Range Assessment of Memory and Learning—Second Edition

The Wide Range Assessment of Memory and Learning—Second Edition is used to assess memory function.

Recognition Subtests	Scaled Score
Story Recognition	1
Design Recognition	1
Verbal Learning Recognition	1
Picture Memory Recognition	1
Index Scores	**Standard Score**
Verbal Recognition	55
Visual Recognition	55
General Recognition	55

Leiter International Performance Scale—Third Edition

The Leiter International Performance Scale—Third Edition (Leiter-3) is a measure of nonverbal intelligence.

Cognitive Subtests	Scale Score	Attention/ Memory	Scale Score
Figure Ground	0	Attention Sustained	0
Form Completion	0	Forward Memory	0
Classification/Analogies Arithmetic	0	Reverse Memory	0
		Nonverbal Stroop Incongruent Correct	0
		Nonverbal Stroop Congruent Correct	5
Cognitive Composite	**Composite Score**	**Percentile**	
Nonverbal IQ	30	<0.1	
Attention/Memory Composite			
Nonverbal Memory	48	<0.1	
Processing Speed	48	<0.1	

Discussion

Results of the neuropsychological evaluation suggest that Daniel is intellectually and psychologically incapable of functioning independently.

Daniel was unable to attend to and perform tasks presented by the examiner. On a measure of adaptive skills, Daniel's mother indicated that his overall level of adaptive functioning was in the Impaired range of functioning. She endorsed only one item indicating that when called by his name, the client was able to move his head toward the sound. No other behaviors or skills were reported by the mother. On a measure of receptive vocabulary, his performance was also within the Impaired range. Daniel fell asleep during the administration. After being called by his name several times, he provided an expressionless stare to his examiner and then drifted away. When redirected toward the presented stimulus, Daniel would either look at the picture for less than five seconds or move his eyes away in an attempt to continue sleeping. No responses were obtained from the client on this test. Similarly, he performed within the Impaired range on a memory test. Daniel was unresponsive throughout the entire administration. He was called by his name and asked to follow an index finger toward a stimulus several times in order to attract his attention. The examiner also touched his hand slightly while calling his name and asked him a question about the stories that were read; however, Daniel's response was limited to a vacant stare toward the wall. On a test of nonverbal intelligence, Daniel's scores fell in the Impaired range as well. He was not able to attend to the visually presented stimulus. He kept looking at the ceiling or toward the wall in spite of being called by his name several times. No responses in the form of eye or head movements were provided when asked about the pictures presented. He was not alert during most part of the administration. In general, Daniel was unable to follow commands and could not stay awake during the administration of the tests. When called by his name, Daniel would respond variably by moving his eyes toward the examiner. However, he would turn away immediately. Daniel has no insight or verbal abilities. He is unresponsive to all forms of communication. Finally, he is incontinent and needs assistance to function in all activities of the daily living.

References

AAIDD (American Association on Intellectual and Developmental Disabilities). 2010. *Intellectual Disability: Definition, classification, and systems of supports.* 11th ed. Washington, DC: American Association on Intellectual and Developmental Disabilities.

APA (American Psychiatric Association). 1952. *Diagnostic and Statistical Manual of Mental Disorders.*

APA (American Psychiatric Association). 1968. *Diagnostic and Statistical Manual of Mental Disorders.* 2nd ed.

APA (American Psychiatric Association). 1980. *Diagnostic and Statistical Manual of Mental Disorders.* 3rd ed.

APA (American Psychiatric Association). 1987. *Diagnostic and Statistical Manual of Mental Disorders.* 3rd ed., text rev.

APA (American Psychiatric Association). 1994. *Diagnostic and Statistical Manual of Mental Disorders.* 4th ed.

APA (American Psychiatric Association). 2013. *Diagnostic and Statistical Manual of Mental Disorders.* 5th ed.

APA (American Psychological Association). 2000. "Report of the Task Force on Test User Qualifications." Retrieved from www.apa.org/science/programs/testing/qualifications.pdf.

Ayres, K.M., L. Mechling, and F.J. Sansosti. 2013. "The Use of Mobile Technologies to Assist with Life Skills/Independence of Students with Moderate/Severe Intellectual Disability and/or Autism Spectrum Disorders: Considerations for the Future of School Psychology." *Psychology in the Schools* 50, no. 3, pp. 259–71.

Bashash, L., L. Outhred, and S. Bochner. 2003. "Counting Skills and Number Concepts of Students with Moderate Intellectual Disabilities." *International Journal of Disability, Development and Education* 50, no. 3, pp. 325–45.

Bauman, M.K. 1974. "Blind and Partially Sighted." In *Psychoeducational Diagnosis of Exceptional Children,* ed. M.V. Wisland, 159–89. Springfield, MA: Carles C. Thomas.

Bayley, N. 1993. *Bayley Scales of Infant Development: Manual.* Psychological Corporation.

Beck, F.W., and J.D. Lindsey. 1986. "Visually Impaired Students' Degree of Visual Acuity and Their Verbal Intelligence Quotients." *Educational & Psychological Research.*

Beirne-Smith, M., J.R. Patton, and S.H. Kim. 2006. *Mental Retardation: An Introduction to Intellectual Disabilities*. Upper Saddle River, NJ: Prentice Hall.

Bernstein, J.H., and D.P. Waber. 1996. *Developmental Scoring System for the Rey-Osterrieth Complex Figure: DSS Rocf*. Psychological Assessment Resources.

Berkson, G. 2004. "Intellectual and Physical Disabilities in Prehistory and Early Civilization." *Mental Retardation* 42, no. 3, pp. 195–208.

Binet, A., and T. Simon. 1913. *A Method of Measuring the Development of the Intelligence of Young Children*. Courier.

Binet, A., and T. Simon. 1916. *The Development of Intelligence in Children: The Binet-Simon Scale*. No. 11. Philadelphia, PA: Williams & Wilkins Company.

Black, D.W., and J.E. Grant. 2014. *DSM-5® Guidebook: The Essential Companion to the Diagnostic and Statistical Manual of Mental Disorders*. Arlington, VA: American Psychiatric Pub.

Bracken, B.A., and R.S. McCallum. 1998. "Universal Nonverbal Intelligence Test."

Braden, J.P. 1994. *Deafness, Deprivation, and IQ*. Berlin, Germany: Springer Science & Business Media.

Braden, J.P., and S.N. Elliott. 2003. *Accommodations on the Stanford-Binet Intelligence Scales*. Itasca, IL: Riverside Publishing.

Braddock, D.L., and S.L. Parish. 2001. "An Institutional History of Disability." In *Handbook of Disability Studies*, eds. G.L. Albrecht, K.D. Seelman, and M. Bury, 11–68. Thousand Oaks, CA: Sage Publications.

Bromberg, W. 1975. *From Shaman to Psychotherapist: A History of the Treatment of Mental Illness*. H. Regnery.

Brown, L., R.J. Sherbenou, and S.K. Johnsen. 2010. *TONI-4, Test of Nonverbal Intelligence*. Pro-Ed.

Carter, E.W., K.L. Lane, M. Cooney, K. Weir, C.K. Moss, and W. Machalicek. 2013. "Parent Assessments of Self-Determination Importance and Performance for Students with Autism or Intellectual Disability." *American Journal on Intellectual and Developmental Disabilities* 118, no. 1, pp. 16–31.

Carvill, S. 2001. "Sensory Impairments, Intellectual Disability and Psychiatry." *Intellectual Disability Research* 45, no. 6, pp. 467–83.

Conners, C.K., and M.H.S. Staff. 2000. *Conners' Continuous Performance Test II (CPT II V. 5)*. North Tonawanda, NY: Multi-Health Systems Inc.

Connolly, A.J. 2007. *KeyMath 3: Diagnostic Assessment*. Bloomington, MN: Pearson.

Crisp, C. 2007. "The Efficacy of Intelligence Testing in Children with Physical Disabilities, Visual Impairments and/or the Inability to Speak." *International Journal of Special Education*. 22, no. 1, pp. 137–41.

Davis, C.J. 1980. *Perkins-Binet tests of Intelligence for the Blind*. Perkins-Binet School for the Blind.

Delis, D.C., J.H. Kramer, E. Kaplan, and B.A. Ober. 1994. *CVLT-C: California Verbal Learning Test.*

Delis, D.C., E. Kaplan, and J.H. Kramer. 2001. *Delis-Kaplan Executive Function System (D-KEFS).* Psychological Corporation.

Dekker, R. 1993. "Visually Impaired Children and Haptic Intelligence Test Scores: Intelligence Test for Visually Impaired Children (ITVIC). *Developmental Medicine & Child Neurology* 35, no. 6, pp. 478–79.

Dunn, L.M., and D.M. Dunn. 2007. *Peabody Picture Vocabulary Test: PPVT 4.* New York: Pearson.

Ferguson, P.M. 2013. "The Development of Systems of Supports: Intellectual Disability in Middle Modern Times (1800 CE to 1899 CE)." In *The Story of Intellectual Disability: An Evolution of Meaning, Understanding, and Public Perception,* ed. M.L. Wehmeyer, 79–115. Baltimore, MD: Paul H. Brookes Publishing Co.

Ferguson, D.L., P.M. Ferguson, and M.L. Wehmeyer. 2013. "The Self-Advocacy Movement: Late Modern Times (1980 CE to Present)." In *The Story of Intellectual Disability: An Evolution of Meaning, Understanding, and Public Perception,* ed. M.L. Wehmeyer, 233–77. Baltimore, MD: Paul H. Brookes Publishing Co.

Ferrell, K.A., S. Bruce, and J.L. Luckner. 2014. "Evidence-Based Practices for Students with Sensory Impairments (Document No. IC-4)." Retrieved from University of Florida, Collaboration for Effective Educator, Development, Accountability, and Reform Center website: http://ceedar.education.ufl.edu/tools/innovation-configurations

Flanagan, D.P., and K.S. McGrew. 1997. "A Cross-Battery Approach to Assessing and Interpreting Cognitive Abilities: Narrowing the Gap Between Practice and Cognitive Science."

Flanagan, D.P., S.O. Ortiz, and V.C. Alfonso. 2013. *Essentials of Cross-Battery Assessment.* Vol. 84. Hoboken, NJ: John Wiley & Sons.

Gazith, K.C. 1997. *Coping Strategies of Children with an Intellectual Disability in Regular Andspecial Classrooms* [Doctoral Dissertation].

Griffiths, R. 1976. *Griffiths Mental Development Scales.* Test Agency.

Golden, C.J. 1978. *Stroop Color and Word Test.* Chicago, IL: Stoelting Company.

Goodman, S.A., G.C. Evans, and M. Loftin. 2011. "Position Paper: Intelligence Testing of Individuals Who Are Blind or Visually Impaired." Louisville, KY: American Printing House for the Blind. *Recuperado em março de.*

Hammill, D.D., N.A. Pearson, and J. Lee Wiederholt. 1997. *Comprehensive Test of Nonverbal Intelligence (CTONI).* Austin, TX: Pro-ed.

Hammill, D.D., and S.C. Larsen. 2009. *Test of Written Language 4 (TOWL-4).* San Antonio, TX: Pearson Assessments.

Harris, J.C. 2006. *Intellectual Disability: Understanding Its Development, Causes, Classification, Evaluation, and Treatment.* New York: Oxford University Press.

Harbour, C.K., and P.K. Maulik. 2010. "History of Intellectual Disability." *International Encyclopaedia of Rehabilitation (online).* Retrieved January 25, 2012 from, http://cirrie.buffalo.edu/encyclopedia/article.php?id=143&language=en

Harrison, P., and T. Oakland. 2003. "Adaptive behavior assessment system (ABAS-II)." San Antonio, TX: The Psychological Corporation.

Heaton, R.K. 1993. "Wisconsin Card Sorting Test: Computer Version 2." Odessa: Psychological Assessment Resources.

Hill-Briggs, F., J.G. Dial, D.A. Morere, and A. Joyce. 2007. "Neuropsychological Assessment of Persons with Physical Disability, Visual Impairment or Blindness, and Hearing Impairment or Deafness." *Archives of Clinical Neuropsychology* 22, no. 3, pp. 389–404.

Hooper, H.E. 1983. *Hooper Visual Organization Test.* Western Psychological Services.

Huntley, M. 1996. "The Griffiths Mental Development Scales: From Birth to 2 Years." *Association for Research in Infant and Child Development (ARICD).*

Hutt, M.L. 1963. *Bender-Gestalt Test.*

Johnson, H., J. Douglas, C. Bigby, and T. Iacono. 2011. "The Challenges and Benefits of Using Participant Observation to Understand the Social Interaction of Adults with Intellectual Disabilities." *Augmentative and Alternative Communication* 27, no. 4, pp. 267–78.

Kamphaus, R.W. 1993. *Clinical Assessment of Children's Intelligence: A Handbook for Professional Practice.* Boston, MA: Allyn & Bacon.

Kaplan, E. 1983. *Boston Diagnostic Aphasia Examination Booklet.* Philadelphia, PA: Lea & Febiger.

Kaplan, E., H. Goodglass, and S. Weintraub. 2001. *Boston Naming Test.* Pro-ed.

Landa-Vialard, O. 2015. "Assessment Considerations for Students Who Are Blind and Visually Impaired." *American Foundation for the Blind Website.* Retrieved November 12, 2015 from, www.afb.org/info/assessment-considerations-for-students-who-are-blind-and-visually-impaired/5#_Toc401239956

Lifshitz, H., S. Shtein, I. Weiss, and N. Svisrsky. 2011. "Explicit Memory Among Individuals with Mild and Moderate Intellectual Disability: Educational Implications." *Journal of Special Needs Education* 26, no. 1, pp. 113–24.

Luria, A.R. 1976. *The Working Brain: An Introduction to Neuropsychology.* Basic Books.

Maulik, P.K., and C.K. Harbour. 2010. "Epidemiology of Intellectual Disability." *International Encyclopaedia of Rehabilitation (online).* Retrieved January 25, 2012 from, http://cirrie.buffalo.edu/encyclopedia/en/article/144/

McGrew, K.S., and D.P. Flanagan. 1998. *The Intelligence Test Desk Reference (ITDR): Gf-Gc Cross-Battery Assessment.* Boston, MA: Allyn & Bacon.

NCES (National Center for Education Statistics). 2012. "Fast Facts." U.S. Department of Education. Retrieved November 12, 2015 from, http://nces.ed.gov/fastfacts/display.asp?id=64

Radford, J.P. 1991. "Sterilization Versus Segregation: Control of the 'Feebleminded,' 1900–1938." *Social Science & Medicine* 33, no. 4, pp. 449–58.

Ramey, C.T., and S.L. Ramey. 1998. "Prevention of Intellectual Disabilities: Early Interventions to Improve Cognitive Development." *Preventive Medicine* 27, no. 2, pp. 224–32.

Reitan, R.M., and D. Wolfson. 1985. *The Halstead-Reitan Neuropsychological Test Battery: Theory and Clinical Interpretation.* Vol. 4. Reitan Neuropsychology.

Roid, G.H., L.J. Miller, and C. Koch. 2013. *Leiter International Performance Scale.* Stoelting.

Ruff, R.M. 1996. *Ruff Figural Fluency Test: Professional Manual.* Psychological Assessment Resources.

Russell, E.W., and M. Levy. 1987. "Revision of the Halstead Category Test." *Journal of Consulting and Clinical Psychology* 55, no. 6, p. 898.

Sansone, S.M., A. Schneider, E. Bickel, E. Berry-Kravis, C. Prescott, and D. Hessl. 2014. "Improving IQ measurement in Intellectual Disabilities Using True Deviation from Population Norms." *Journal of Neurodevelopmental Disorders* 6, no. 1, p. 1.

Sattler, J.M. 2008. *Assessment of Children: Cognitive Foundations.* La Mesa, CA: JM Sattler.

Sattler, J.M., and J.J. Ryan. 2009. *Assessment with the WAIS-IV.* La Mesa, CA: Jerome M Sattler Publisher.

Schalock, R.L., R.A. Luckasson, and K.A. Shogren. 2007. "The Renaming of Mental Retardation: Understanding the Change to the Term Intellectual Disability." *Intellectual and Developmental Disabilities* 45, no. 2, pp. 116–24.

Schalock, R.L., S.A. Borthwick-Duffy, V.J. Bradley, W.H.E. Buntinx, D.L. Coulter, E.M. Craig, and M.H. Yeager. 2010. *Intellectual Disability: Definition, Classification and Systems of Supports American Association on Intellectual and Developmental Disabilities.* Washington, DC.

Schalock, R.L., and R. Luckasson. 2013. "What's at Stake in the Lives of People with Intellectual Disability? Part I: The Power of Naming, Defining, Diagnosing, Classifying, and Planning Supports." *Intellectual and Developmental Disabilities* 51, no. 2, pp. 86–93.

Sheslow, D., and W. Adams. 2003. "Wide Range Assessment of Memory and Learning–Revised (WRAML-2). Administration and Technical Manual. Wide Range." Inc.: Wilmington, DE.

Shine, A.E., and T. Vaccario. 2004. "Mental Retardation: A Primer for Parents." Retrieved from The National Association of School Psychologists.

Shrank, E.A., V. Mather, and K.S. McGrew. 2014. *Woodcock=Johnson IV Tests of Achievement*. Rolling Meadows, IL: Riverside.

Slosson, R.L., C.L. Nicholson, and T.H. Hibpshman. 1991. *Slosson Intelligence Test, Revised (SIT-R3)*. Austin, TX: Slosson Education Publications.

Smith, K.A., S.B. Shepley, J.L. Alexander, and K.M. Ayres. 2015. "The Independent Use of Self-Instructions for the Acquisition of Untrained Multi-Step Tasks for Individuals with an Intellectual Disability: A Review of the Literature." *Research in Developmental Disabilities* 40, pp. 19–30.

Sofair, A.N., and L.C. Kaldjian. 2000. "Eugenic Sterilization and a Qualified Nazi analogy: The United States and Germany, 1930–1945." *Annals of Internal Medicine* 132, no. 4, pp. 312–19.

Sparrow, S.S., D.V. Cicchetti, and D.A. Balla. 2005. "Vineland Adaptive Behavior Scales: (Vineland II), Survey Interview Form/Caregiver Rating Form." Livonia, MN: Pearson Assessments.

Tiffin, J. 1968. *Purdue Pegboard Examiner Manual*. Science Research Associates.

Timmons, J.C., A.C. Hall, J. Bose, A. Wolfe, and J. Winsor. 2011. "Choosing Employment: Factors that Impact Employment Decisions for Individuals with Intellectual Disability." *Intellectual and Developmental Disabilities* 49, no. 4, pp. 285–99.

Thorndike, R.L., E.P. Hagen, and J.M. Sattler. 1986. *Stanford-Binet Intelligence Scale*. Rolling Meadows, IL: Riverside Publishing Company.

Trites, R. 1989. "Grooved Pegboard Test." Lafayette, Ind.: Lafayette Instrument.

U.S. Department of Education. 2014. Office of Special Education and Rehabilitative Services, Office of Special Education Programs. *36th Annual Report to Congress of the Implemenation of the Individuals with Disabilities Education Act*. Washington, DC: Author.

Vig, S., and M. Sanders. 2007. "Assessment of Mental Retardation." *Preschool Assessment: Principles and Practices*, pp. 420–47.

Watkins, M.W., E.A. Youngstrom, and J.J. Glutting. 2002. "Some Cautions Concerning Cross-Battery Assessment." *NASP Communiqué* 30, no. 5, pp. 15–20.

Wechsler, D. 2006. *Wechsler Nonverbal Scale of Ability: WNV*. Edited by Franz Petermann. PsychCorp.

Wechsler, D. 2009. *Wechsler Memory Scale-(WMS-IV)*. New York: The Psychological Corporation.

Wechsler, D. 2012. *Wechsler Preschool and Primary Schools of Intelligence-WPPSI-IV*. San Antonio, TX: Pearson.

Wechsler, D. 2014. *Wechsler Intelligence Scale for Children-WISC-V*. San Antonio, TX: Pearson.

Wechsler, D., D.L. Coalson, and S.E. Raiford. 2008. *WAIS-IV: Wechsler Adult Intelligence Scale*. San Antonio, TX: Pearson.

Wehmeyer, M.L., S. Noll, and J.D. Smith. 2013. "Isolation, Enlargement, Economization: Intellectual Disability in Late Modern Times (1930 CE to 1950 CE)." In *The Story of Intellectual Disability: An Evolution of Meaning, Understanding and Public Perception,* ed. M.L. Wehmeyer, 157–185. Baltimore, MD: Paul H. Brookes Publishing Co.

Wehmeyer, M.L., and S. Lee. 2007. "Educating Children with Intellectual Disability and Autism-Spectrum Disorders." In *The Handbook of Intellectual Disability and Clinical Psychology Practice*, eds. A. Car, G. O-Reily, P.N. Walsh, and J. McEvoy, 559–605. New York: Taylor & Francis Group.

Wickham, P. 2013. "Poverty and the Emergence of Charity: Intellectual Disability in the Middle Ages (500 C.E. to 1500 C.E.)." In *The Story of Intellectual Disability: An Evolution of Meaning, Understanding and Public Perception,* ed. M.L. Wehmeyer, 47–62. Baltimore, MD: Paul H. Brookes Publishing Co.

Wilhoit, B.E., and R.S. McCallum. 2003. "Cross-Battery Assessment of Nonverbal Cognitive Ability." In *Handbook of nonverbal assessment*, 63–83. New York: Springer US.

Wilkinson, G.S., and G.J. Robertson. 2006. *Wide Range Achievement Test—Fourth Edition*. Lutz, FL: Psychological Assessment Resources.

Wilson, D.N., and A. Haire. 1990. "Health Care Screening for People with Mental Handicap Living in the Community." *BMJ* 301, no. 6765, pp. 1379–81.

World Health Organization. 1992. *The ICD-10 Classification of Mental and Behavioural Disorders: Descriptions and Diagnostic Guidelines*. Geneva, Switzerland: World Health Organization.

Index

AAIDD. *See* American Association
of Intellectual and
Developmental Disabilities
ABAS-II. *See* Adaptive Behavior
Rating Scale-Second Edition
Academic accommodations
for students with intellectual
disability, 63–69
in vocational settings, 69–70
Achievement tests
Key Math-3 Diagnostic
Assessment, 44
overview of, 42–43
Wide Range Achievement Test-
Fourth Edition, 43
Woodcock-Johnson Tests of
Achievement-Fourth Edition,
43
Adaptive Behavior Assessment Scale-
Second Edition, 96
Adaptive Behavior Assessment
System-Second Edition, 125
Adaptive Behavior Rating Scale-
Second Edition (ABAS-II)
administration, 41–42
interpretation, 42
limitations, 42
overview of, 41
standardization, 42
Adaptive functioning, assessment of,
50
American Association of Intellectual
and Developmental
Disabilities (AAIDD), 29–30
Assessments for the blind, 57–59
Assessments for the deaf, 51–57

Battelle Developmental Inventory,
Second Edition, 118–120
Beery-Buktenica Developmental Test
of Visual-Motor Integration,
Sixth Edition, 93

Borderline intellectual functioning
behavioral observations, 73–74
Conners' Continuous Performance
Test II, 77
Conners 3 Parent Rating Scales,
79–82
definition, 2
discussion results, 85–87
Expressive Vocabulary Test-Second
Edition, 75
Finger Tapping Test, 78
history of the problem, 71–73
Key Math 3, 77
mental status exam, 73
Personality Inventory for Children-
Second Edition, 83–85
Personality Inventory for Youth,
82–83
Test of Memory Malingering, 85
Trail Making Tests A and B, 78–79
Wechsler Intelligence Scale for
Children-Fifth Edition, 74
Wide Range Assessment of
Memory and Learning-
Second Edition, 75–76
Wisconsin Card Sorting Test, 78
Woodcock-Johnson Tests of
Achievement-Third Edition,
76–77
Brain
primary areas of, 7–8
secondary areas of, 8–11
tertiary areas of, 12–13

Category Test, 106, 114–115
Conners' Continuous Auditory Test
of Attention, 105, 113–114
Conners' Continuous Performance
Test II, 77, 113
Conners' Continuous Performance
Test III, 104
Conners' 3 Parent Rating Scales,
79–82, 93–95

Diagnostic and Statistical Manual of
Mental Disorders (DSM)
DSM-5, 21–24
DSM-I, 17–18
DSM-II, 18–19
DSM-III, 19–20
DSM-III-R, 19–20
DSM-IV, 21
DSM-IV-TR, 21
history of, 17

EVT. *See* Expressive Vocabulary Test
Expressive Vocabulary Test (EVT),
104
Second Edition, 75, 92

Finger Tapping Test, 78, 107

General intelligence, 5
Generalized assessments, 30–31

ICD-10. *See* International Statistical
Classification of Diseases and
Related Health Problems
Individuals with motor impairments
assessments, 59–60
Intellectual disability
borderline intellectual functioning,
2
definition, 1–2
differential diagnoses, 24–25
DSM and, 17–24
etiology of, 13
history and sociocultural
background, 13–16
mild, 2–3
moderate, 3
nomenclature, 1–2
profound, 4
severe, 3–4
severity and diagnosis, 2
Intelligence, measures of, 30–31
Intelligence quotient (IQ), 6–7
International Statistical Classification
of Diseases and Related
Health Problems (ICD-10),
27–29

IQ. *See* Intelligence quotient

Key Math 3, 77
Key Math-3 Diagnostic Assessment
(KM-3 DA), 44
KM-3 DA. *See* Key Math-3
Diagnostic Assessment

Leiter International Performance
Scale-Third Edition, 38–39,
126

Measures of intelligence, 30–31
Mild intellectual disability
Adaptive Behavior Assessment
Scale-Second Edition, 96
Beery-Buktenica Developmental
Test of Visual-Motor
Integration, Sixth Edition, 93
behavioral observations, 88–89,
101
Category Test, 106
Conners' Continuous Auditory Test
of Attention, 105
Conners' Continuous Performance
Test III, 104
Conners' 3 Parent Rating Scales,
93–95
diagnosis of, 2–3
discussion results, 96–98, 107–108
Expressive Vocabulary Test, 104
Expressive Vocabulary Test-Second
Edition, 92
Finger Tapping Test, 107
history of the problem, 87–88,
98–100
mental status exam, 88, 100–101
Peabody Picture Vocabulary Test-
Fourth Edition, 92–93, 104
Personality Inventory for Children-
Second Edition, 95–96
school observations, 89
Tactual Performance Test, 106–107
Test of Memory Malingering, 107
Trail Making Tests A and B, 106
Wechsler Adult Intelligence Scale-
Fourth Edition, 101–102

Wechsler Memory Scale-Fourth
    Edition, 103
Wechsler Preschool and Primary
    Scale of Intelligence-Fourth
    Edition, 90
Wide Range Assessment of
    Memory and Learning-
    Second Edition, 90–91
Wisconsin Card Sorting Test,
    105–106
Woodcock-Johnson Cognitive-
    Third Edition, 102
Woodcock-Johnson IV Test of
    Cognitive Abilities, 91
Woodcock-Johnson Tests of
    Achievement-Fourth Edition,
    92
Woodcock-Johnson Tests of
    Achievement-Third Edition,
    103
Moderate intellectual disability
    Battelle Developmental Inventory,
        Second Edition, 118–120
    Category Test, 114–115
    Conners' CATA, 113–114
    Conners' Continuous Performance
        Test II, 113
    diagnosis of, 3
    discussion results, 115–116,
        120–123
    history of the problem, 109–110,
        117–118
    Peabody Picture Vocabulary Test,
        Fourth Edition, 113
    Stanford Binet Intelligence Scales-
        Fifth Edition, 110
    Stroop Color-Word Test, 115
    Test of Memory Malingering, 115
    Wechsler Memory Scale-Fourth
        Edition, 111
    Wide Range Achievement Test-
        Fourth Edition, 112
    Wisconsin Card Sorting Test, 114
    Woodcock-Johnson Tests of
        Achievement-Fourth Edition,
        112

Woodcock Johnson Tests of
    Cognitive Abilities-Fourth
    Edition, 111
Modern nonverbal intelligence
    measures, 57
Modern verbal intelligence measures,
    59

Nonverbal intelligence assessments
    Leiter International Performance
        Scale-Third Edition, 38–39
    Peabody Picture Vocabulary Test-
        Fourth Edition, 39
    Test of Nonverbal Intelligence-
        Fourth Edition, 37–38
    Universal Nonverbal Intelligence
        Test, 34–37
    Wechsler Nonverbal Scale of
        Ability, 40

Occupational learning, 68–69

Peabody Picture Vocabulary Test-
    Fourth Edition (PPVT-4), 39,
    92–93, 104, 113, 125
Personality Inventory for Children-
    Second Edition (PIC-2),
    83–85, 95–96
Personality Inventory for Youth,
    82–83
Persons with intellectual disabilities
    and sensory impairments
    assessment, 45–50
    assessment of adaptive functioning,
        50
    guidelines for report writing, 51
    training and experience, 50–51
PIC-2. See Personality Inventory for
    Children-Second Edition
PPVT-4. See Peabody Picture
    Vocabulary Test-Fourth
    Edition
Primary skills, 7–8
Profound intellectual disability, 4

Report writing, guidelines for, 51

Secondary skills, 8–11
Severe intellectual disability
  Adaptive Behavior Assessment
    System-Second Edition, 125
  behavioral observations, 124
  discussion results, 126–127
  history of the problem, 123–124
  Leiter International Performance
    Scale-Third Edition, 126
  mental status exam, 124
  overview of, 3–4
  Peabody Picture Vocabulary Test-
    Fourth Edition, 125
  Wide Range Assessment of
    Memory and Learning-
    Second Edition, 125–126
Social and coping skills, 67–68
Stanford Binet Intelligence Scales-
  Fifth Edition (SB-5), 110
Stroop Color-Word Test, 115
Students with intellectual disability,
    academic accommodations
  general accommodations, 64–65
  mathematics, 68
  occupational learning, 68–69
  overview of, 63
  presentation mode, 66–67
  social and coping skills, 67–68
  technology, 65–66

Tactual Performance Test, 106–107
Tertiary skills, 12–13
Test of Memory Malingering
  (TOMM), 85, 107, 115
Test of Nonverbal Intelligence-Fourth
  Edition (TONI-4), 37–38
Tests of Adaptive Functioning. *See*
  Adaptive Behavior Rating
  Scale-Second Edition
  (ABAS-II)
TOMM. *See* Test of Memory
  Malingering
TONI-4. *See* Test of Nonverbal
  Intelligence-Fourth Edition
Trail Making Tests A and B, 78–79,
  106

UNIT. *See* Universal Nonverbal
  Intelligence Test
Universal Nonverbal Intelligence Test
  (UNIT), 34–37
  administration, 35–36
  interpretation, 36
  limitations, 37
  overview of, 34–35
  standardization, 36–37

Verbal intelligence assessments
  Wechsler Adult Intelligence Scale-
    Fourh Edition, 33–34
  Wechsler Intelligence Scale for
    Children-Fifth Edition,
    31–32
Vocational settings, academic
  accommodations, 69–70

WAIS-IV. *See* Wechsler Adult
  Intelligence Scale-Fourh
  Edition
Wechsler Adult Intelligence Scale-
  Fourh Edition (WAIS-IV),
  101–102
  administration, 33
  interpretation, 33–34
  limitations, 34
  overview of, 33
  standardization, 34
Wechsler Intelligence Scale for
  Children-Fifth Edition
  (WISC-V), 74
  administration, 32
  interpretation, 32
  limitations, 33
  overview of, 31
  standardization, 32–33
Wechsler Memory Scale-Fourth
  Edition, 103, 111
Wechsler Nonverbal Scale of Ability
  (WNV), 40
Wechsler Preschool and Primary
  Scale of Intelligence-Fourth
  Edition, 90

Wide Range Achievement Test-Fourth Edition (WRAT-4), 43, 112

Wide Range Assessment of Memory and Learning-Second Edition, 75–76, 90–91, 125–126

Wisconsin Card Sorting Test, 78, 105–106, 114

WISC-V. *See* Wechsler Intelligence Scale for Children-Fifth Edition

WJ-Ach 4. *See* Woodcock-Johnson Tests of Achievement-Fourth Edition

Woodcock-Johnson Cognitive-Third Edition, 102

Woodcock-Johnson Tests of Achievement-Fourth Edition (WJ-Ach 4), 43, 92, 112

Woodcock-Johnson Tests of Achievement-Third Edition, 76–77, 103

Woodcock Johnson Tests of Cognitive Abilities-Fourth Edition, 91, 111

WRAT-4. *See* Wide Range Achievement Test-Fourth Edition

FORTHCOMING TITLES FOR THIS CHILD CLINICAL PSYCHOLOGY "NUTS AND BOLTS" COLLECTION

Samuel T. Gontkovsky, *Editor*

Childhood Sleep Disorders
By Connie J. Schnoes

A Guide to Statistics for the Behavioral Sciences
By Jeff Foster

Bipolar and Related Disorders in Children and Adolescents
By Elizabeth B. Hamilton

Childhood Autism Spectrum Disorders
By Jessica Glass Kendorski

Motor Disorders in Children
By Omar Rahman

Elimination Disorders
By Thomas Reimers

Momentum Press is one of the leading book publishers in the field of engineering, mathematics, health, and applied sciences. Momentum Press offers over 30 collections, including Aerospace, Biomedical, Civil, Environmental, Nanomaterials, Geotechnical, and many others.

Momentum Press is actively seeking collection editors as well as authors. For more information about becoming an MP author or collection editor, please visit
http://www.momentumpress.net/contact

Announcing Digital Content Crafted by Librarians

Momentum Press offers digital content as authoritative treatments of advanced engineering topics by leaders in their field. Hosted on ebrary, MP provides practitioners, researchers, faculty, and students in engineering, science, and industry with innovative electronic content in sensors and controls engineering, advanced energy engineering, manufacturing, and materials science.

Momentum Press offers library-friendly terms:

- perpetual access for a one-time fee
- no subscriptions or access fees required
- unlimited concurrent usage permitted
- downloadable PDFs provided
- free MARC records included
- free trials

The **Momentum Press** digital library is very affordable, with no obligation to buy in future years.

For more information, please visit **www.momentumpress.net/library** or to set up a trial in the US, please contact **mpsales@globalepress.com**.

www.ingramcontent.com/pod-product-compliance
Lightning Source LLC
Chambersburg PA
CBHW050529270326
41926CB00015B/3143